Natural Resources and the State

STUDIES IN INTERNATIONAL POLITICAL ECONOMY

Edited by Stephen D. Krasner
Department of Political Science
University of California
Los Angeles

Albert O. Hirschman, *National Power and the Structure of Foreign Trade*

Robert A. Pastor, *Congress and the Politics of U.S. Foreign Economic Policy 1929-1976*

Oran R. Young, *Natural Resources and the State: The Political Economy of Resource Management*

Natural Resources and the State

The Political Economy of Resource Management

Oran R. Young

University of California Press
Berkeley   Los Angeles   London

University of California Press
Berkeley and Los Angeles, California

University of California Press, Ltd.
London, England

Library of Congress Cataloging in Publication Data

Young, Oran R.
  Natural resources and the state.

  (Studies in international political economy)
  Includes bibliographical references and index.
  1. Environmental policy.   2. Natural resources.
3. Environmental policy—Alaska.   4. Natural resources
—Alaska.   I. Title.   II. Series.
HC79.E5Y68   333.7   80-25951
ISBN 0-520-04285-9

Printed in the United States of America

1 2 3 4 5 6 7 8 9

To Gail, valued companion in many realms

Contents

Preface

This volume reflects an effort to integrate three distinct lines of enquiry. For many years, I have been interested in various theories of the state, classical as well as contemporary. Although the reader will soon find that I am a confirmed skeptic concerning most claims made on behalf of the state, I do not consider myself a representative of any single school of thought regarding either the actual or the proper role of the state. More recently, I have turned my attention increasingly to an effort to improve our understanding of the ways in which society makes decisions about the use of natural resources. Given the rather primitive quality of the literature on the politics of natural resources, it was only natural for me to have drawn on my work in the field of theories of the state in attempting to come to terms with the political economy of resource management. Even more specifically, I have been endeavoring for some time to comprehend the problems of the far North in the contemporary era. Since many of these problems revolve around the use of natural resources, I have drawn extensively on my work in the far North as a source of case materials pertaining to the state and natural resources. To the extent that this work has merit, I believe it stems from the effort to integrate these several lines of enquiry into a coherent argument offering theoretical insights as well as empirical details.

My work on this project was made possible by the helpful responses I received from numerous individuals and, simultaneously, made difficult by the bureaucratic responses of several governmental agencies. Individuals who were supportive are too numerous to mention by name. Thus I owe a substantial debt of gratitude to the officers and men of the U.S. Coast Guard Cutters *Jarvis* and *Munro*, with which I sailed on fisheries patrol in 1978 and 1979. I was extremely well received by many individuals, both Native and nonNative, in the communities of Saint Paul and Saint George, where I studied the commercial harvest of northern fur seals in 1979. And I have had constructive discussions over a period of several years with several people associated with corporations created under the terms of the Alaska Native Claims Settlement Act, though I have made no attempt to hide my doubts about the performance and impact of these corporations. Additionally, I am grateful to various colleagues who have read drafts of portions of this work and argued with me about the issues raised, as well as to the outside reviewers engaged by the University of California Press who stimulated me to rethink several questions pertaining to the organization of this volume. While final responsibility for the contents of the work obviously rests with me, there is no doubt that this project could hardly have materialized without the tolerance and generally supportive attitudes of many of these people.

The support I received from individuals takes on special significance in the light of the problems of dealing with governmental agencies to which I alluded above. A study of natural resources and the state, with particular reference to the American experience, could hardly proceed in the absence of regular contact with various federal agencies. But unfortunately, relations between independent scholars and governmental agencies are fraught with difficulties. The agencies are typically preoccupied with bureaucratic routines, worried about internal or institutional political battles, and generally lacking in any sense of how to make constructive use of independent scholars. The scholars, for their part, are often unable or unwilling to comprehend the institutional problems of the agencies and unprepared for the bureaucratic routines that are commonplace in the agencies. Over and over again, this results in mutual incomprehension coupled with an attitude of indifference on the part of agency personnel. In my experience, the resultant impediment to serious research on public policy can only be ameliorated with almost infinite patience and can probably never be overcome completely.

My work on this project, however, has convinced me of the importance of efforts to establish and maintain meaningful contact between independent scholars and agency personnel. Contact with the real world is obviously a useful antidote to the academic musings of many scholars. But some willingness to interact with independent scholars is equally important in countering the tendency of agency personnel to lose track of the larger issues facing society and to become preoccupied with the trivial details of institutional politics. While I have no magic formula for the pursuit of this objective, I am persuaded that we should all make a good faith effort to keep these lines of communication open.

O. R. Y.

Washington, D.C.
June 1980

One

The Role of the State

In the United States, the federal government retains ownership of approximately one-third of the land, despite the existence of vigorous programs aimed at transferring land and
other natural resources into private hands during much of the
nation's history.[1] Virtually all the wild animals in America
belong to the state and fall under the jurisdiction of one or
more levels of government. The state owns more than half of
the standing stock of softwood timber in the nation.[2] All
efforts to exploit oil and gas on the outer continental shelves
adjacent to the United States must conform to the requirements of an explicit regime promulgated by the federal
government (or by various state governments inside the
three-mile limit).[3] And it would be easy to enumerate
additional examples of the involvement of the state in this
realm. It follows that the state cannot avoid playing a central
role in arriving at societal decisions about the use of natural
resources in the United States. But what should the character
and content of this role be? What objectives should the state
pursue with respect to the use of natural resources, and what
have been the consequences of various strategies relating to
natural resources actually pursued by the state from time to
time? A study of these questions will not only shed light on

the political economy of resource management, it will also yield interesting observations of a more general sort about the position of the state in contemporary societies. Not surprisingly, there are several distinct perspectives from which to approach these questions. Without doubt, the most fully developed and powerful of these perspectives is the work of economists treating natural resources as a form of social capital and arguing that the proper way to think about the use of these resources is in terms of the analytic structure of neoclassical microeconomics.[4] Two powerful assumptions lie at the heart of this microeconomic perspective on natural resources. There is, in the first instance, the assumption that decisions concerning the use of natural resources are typically made by private individuals or corporations seeking to maximize their own welfare through the operation of competitive markets and that these processes ordinarily yield allocations of resources approximating the social optimum. These ideas are exemplified in Scott's statement that "I shall (initially) adopt the point of view that society divides its resources and factors between conservation and depletion, investment and consumption according to the plans of individuals, entrepreneurs and households, and that through the operation of the market this allocation is the social optimum."[5] In dealing with natural resources, therefore, it is only necessary to *supplement* market interactions to cope with occasional market failures arising from such phenomena as social costs (or externalities), nonexcludability, and common property.

It follows directly from this assumption that public authorities or governments should and generally will confine themselves in the realm of natural resources to a role of correcting or supplementing market transactions, avoiding (wherever possible) deep intrusions into the workings of the relevant market mechanisms.[6] The result is an application of the liberal theory of the state in which the proper role of government is conceptualized in terms of securing and facilitating the operation of the private sector rather than playing a more active or directive role in arriving at social choices concerning the use of natural resources.[7] This sets the stage for a second powerful assumption embedded in the microeconomic perspective. In cases where there is a supplemental role for government, microeconomic analyses generally assume both that the state is capable of operating as a purposive, integrated actor choosing among alternatives in a rational fashion and that it is motivated primarily by the goal of achieving social optimality defined largely in terms of allocative efficiency. This premise, too, is exemplified by Scott when he asserts that "it is the assumption of this study that the legislature can and should make policies which tend toward the same absolute maximum that could be achieved in the simpler model economy."[8]

An alternative framework to guide thinking about the use of natural resources can be described as the ecological perspective. The influence of this point of view has expanded rapidly in recent years with the growth of environmentalism within the policymaking community as well as among the general public. The use of natural resources, according to the ecological perspective, must be thought of in terms of the interplay of complex ecosystems and the first law of ecology that asserts that everything is connected to everything else.[9] Consequently, it is important to be sensitive at all times to the dangers of generating environmental impacts or external intrusions into individual ecosystems that have the effect of degrading their "natural capacity for self-adjustment."[10] Unfortunately, the free enterprise system prevailing in countries like the United States does not provide adequate incentives for individual actors to minimize or to regulate the generation of environmental impacts.[11] This is partly attributable to the pervasiveness of spillovers or social costs affecting ecosystems and to the absence or undeveloped nature of private property rights in ecosystems as such. In part, it is because the maintenance of ecosystems typically requires the provision of collective goods and because there are well-known barriers to the supply of collective goods in predominantly free enterprise systems.[12]

It follows from this line of reasoning that there is a need for the state to step in to protect the ecosphere and maintain ecological balance. Interestingly, this framework shares with the microeconomic perspective the assumption that the state or the government can be treated as a purposive, integrated actor capable of choosing among alternatives in a generally rational fashion. But the two approaches diverge from this point onward. Thus, the ecological perspective suggests that the state should be guided by the dictates of maintaining ecological balance in contrast to the requirements of achieving allocative efficiency.[13] Additionally, this perspective quickly leads to the conclusion that it is necessary to go beyond the liberal conception of the state as a modest actor endeavoring to correct for occasional market failures and to contemplate a more activist state taking vigorous steps to protect the ecosphere from the ravages that are an inevitable, though often unintended, result of the unrestricted operation of a free enterprise system. In effect, the ecological perspective suggests that man should adopt an attitude of stewardship in dealing with the natural environment and that the role of steward must be assumed primarily by governmental agencies.

What do states actually do that affects society's decisions about the use of natural resources? The perspectives I have outlined in the preceding paragraphs tend to dispose of this question by assumption. But the assumptions they make are often easier to understand as expressions of normative preferences than as propositions with empirical content. And to the extent that these assumptions are intended to have empirical content, they typically appear to reflect wishful thinking and to lead to propositions bearing little resemblance to real-world conditions. At the same time, professional students of politics have seldom turned their attention to the role of the state in the realm of natural resources.[14] The result is an intellectual vacuum concerning the politics of natural resources. Whatever its other strengths, therefore, a major deficiency in the growing literature on natural resources and environmental quality is a general lack of sophistication regarding the nature of the state and the capabilities of government. This constitutes the backdrop for the present collection of essays. My purpose in conducting the research reported in this volume has been to take some initial steps toward increasing the sophistication of our thinking about the role of the state in the realm of natural resources.

A little reflection makes it clear that the state can pursue any of several differentiable strategies regarding the use of natural resources. Without undue distortion, these strategies can be grouped into three basic families, which I shall label devolution, operation, and regulation. The essential idea behind *devolution* is that it is desirable to transfer natural resources (including land) from the public domain into private hands, relying primarily on the operation of competitive markets in arriving at social choices concerning the use of these resources. *Operation,* by contrast, occurs when the state simply steps in and sets itself up as an operating authority with a monopoly over the use of various natural resources. The underlying premise here is that it is preferable to have major decisions concerning the use of natural resources made in the public sector rather than entrusting them to the actions of large numbers of individuals or corporations operating in the private sector. These two families of strategies constitute the traditional grand alternatives in discussions of the proper role of the state in numerous functional areas. Beyond this, however, *regulation* comes into play where there are compelling reasons to conclude that the actions of private individuals or corporations in using natural resources (whether these resources are privately owned or merely made available for private use by the state) will not yield socially optimal results. Under the circumstances, regulation involves intervention on the part of the state to restrict the activities of private actors or to alter their incentives with respect to the use of natural resources. Of course, these several types of strategies are not always mutually exclusive. For example, there is nothing to prevent the state from pursuing a policy of transferring natural resources into private hands but taking steps to regulate more or less closely what private actors can do with these resources at the same time.[15] Similarly, it is perfectly possible for the state to create operating authorities to deal with some natural resources even while taking steps to transfer others into private hands. Nonetheless, it seems fair to conclude that these three families of strategies encompass the major approaches available to the state in attempting to come to terms with specific problems in the realm of natural resources.

The empirical chapters of this volume are organized in such a way as to permit detailed explorations of the behavior of the state in connection with each of these families of strategies. The emphasis is on actual cases drawn from American experiences in the realm of natural resources in contrast to the formulation of normative theory. It should be obvious, however, that outcomes occurring under real-world conditions may have far-reaching normative implications, and I certainly draw attention to these implications as my analysis progresses. Perhaps it is also worth emphasizing that the cases I have chosen to pursue in depth are merely illustrative. While I am convinced that they are representative of larger classes of problems in the realm of natural resources policy, it is evident that an examination of such cases can only suggest insights or raise hypotheses. I am under no illusion that this exercise will permit us to draw definitive conclusions about the performance of the state in the realm of natural resources.

DEVOLUTION

For one reason or another, modern states have generally found themselves in possession of large segments of their societies' lands and natural resources. Sometimes this has occurred as a consequence of inheritances from the days of monarchical government. In other cases, it has resulted either from the acquisition of additional territory by the state or from the changes brought about by a far-reaching social revolution. Whatever the origins of this situation, many states have responded to it by initiating extensive programs designed to transfer land and other natural resources into private hands. In most cases, the philosophical justification for such programs lies in the precepts of liberal capitalism. The individual is the key element of society, and private ownership of land and natural resources can be expected to contribute to the development of human dignity and the maintenance of political freedom.[16] The spirit of free enterprise is a powerful force that can be expected to lead to the emergence of competitive markets in natural resources, which will, in turn, yield socially optimal results with respect to the use of these resources. Under the circumstances, the state should confine itself to a modest role, correcting for occasional market failures but avoiding a more active part in making decisions about the use of natural resources. It follows that states finding themselves in possession of large quantities of land and natural resources should devise clear and effective programs aimed at transferring these resources into private hands.

In the United States, the federal government came into possession of large segments of the society's lands and natural resources through a combination of purchase (for example, the Louisiana Purchase and the purchase of Alaska), organized coercion directed toward other states (for example, the Southwest), negotiated settlement (for example, the Pacific Northwest), and unilateral proclamation (for example, the outer continental shelves). Not surprisingly, these acquisitions have led to vigorous programs designed to transfer natural resources into private hands. Two major types of programs evolved in this context. To begin with, many programs have emphasized the formal conveyance of land and all associated natural resources to private actors through some form of patenting. Obvious examples include the Northwest Ordinance, the Homestead Act, and various

grants of land to individual states for subsequent distribution
to private individuals. While such programs constituted a
prominent feature of life in America during the nineteenth
century, they began to die out early in the twentieth century.[17] With a few exceptions (for example, the grant of
approximately 104 million acres to the state of Alaska in
1958), this practice has not been a central feature of resource
management in the United States for some time.

The federal government, however, has come to rely
increasingly on programs designed to transfer into private
hands important rights to natural resources under federal
jurisdiction without conveying the full rights of ownership to
the recipients. Clearcut examples here include the development of water rights (particularly in the West), grazing rights
on federally owned range land, and leasing systems giving
private individuals or corporations the right to harvest timber
or exploit oil and natural gas under federal jurisdiction.[18]
While certain aspects of this practice are controversial, there is
no sign that it is declining as a means of transferring natural
resources into private hands in the United States. On the contrary, new rights of this type are still emerging (for example,
rights to resources on the outer continental shelves or the
deep seabed), while established rights of this type show few
signs of disappearing.

The case study of devolution I have chosen for inclusion
in this volume deals with lands and natural resources in
Alaska and focuses on the policies reflected in the Alaska
Native Claims Settlement Act of 1971 (PL 92–203; 85 Stat.
688, 43 USC 1601 et seq.).[19] All 375 million acres of land in
Alaska were conveyed to the federal government of the
United States by Russia in the Treaty of Cession of 1867 (UST
301), and the federal government proceeded to administer
this land as a matter of sovereign right. Nevertheless, much
of the land was also occupied by various groups of Native
peoples who had never been conquered by the American
government and who had never entered into any treaties or

other agreements with the United States relinquishing their claims to land in Alaska. This combination of circumstances gave rise to the Alaska Native claims problem. Accordingly, the purpose of PL 92-203 was to provide a definitive resolution of this situation. Specifically, the Act calls for the formal conveyance of 43.7 million acres of land to the Native peoples of Alaska in various forms (together with a substantial monetary settlement) in return for an agreement on the part of these peoples to relinquish all outstanding claims to land or compensation arising either from "aboriginal title in Alaska based on use and occupancy" (sec. 4[b]) or from any previous treaties or statutes.[20] As such, the Native Claims Settlement Act involves what is arguably the largest single act of devolution in American history with respect to lands and natural resources.[21]

OPERATION

As an alternative to devolution, the state can simply proceed to set itself up as an operating authority controlling the use of various natural resources. Ultimately, the philosophical basis of this strategy lies in socialist ideas about the desirability of public ownership of major forms of social capital as well as the means of production.[22] But it does not require a comprehensive shift to socialism to argue that the state should serve as an operating authority in dealing with some natural resources. Thus, many states that have certainly not experienced a full-fledged transition to socialism (for example, the United Kingdom and Canada) have found it expedient to set up national oil companies. Additionally, numerous variations on the theme of the state as operating authority are possible. Public representation on the boards of directors of corporations active in the realm of natural resources can be arranged. For example, the British government has long maintained representation on the board of directors of British Petroleum.[23] Alternatively, the state can experiment with various forms of mixed ownership, forming consortia in which both the state and private entities participate at the same time. This option is exemplified by Panarctic Oils, Ltd. in Canada, a consortium composed of the state oil company (Petro-Canada) together with a large number of private firms. Yet another arrangement is for the state to create public corporations dealing with natural resources under relatively loose governmental supervision. This option is prominently represented by the Tennessee Valley Authority (TVA) in the United States, a public corporation that has succeeded in assembling a substantial natural resource empire.

On the whole, the strategy labeled operation has not been employed extensively in the United States. The TVA is of course a salient exception, but even modest proposals for additional movement in this direction (for example, the suggestion that the federal government undertake exploratory work in connection with outer continental shelf oil and gas development) are seldom met with much enthusiasm in the American political and economic systems. By contrast, this strategy has been followed regularly by other states, including many that are hardly socialist in any thoroughgoing sense. This is especially true in the realm of energy where state oil companies are commonplace. Thus, we now have Petro-Canada in Canada, the British National Oil Company (BNOC) in the United Kingdom, Statoil in Norway, Pemex in Mexico, and so forth. But public operating authorities are by no means uncommon in other areas such as mining, transportation, and the use of water resources. Beyond this, the state has obviously set itself up as an operating authority with respect to natural resources in the countries of the Soviet bloc as well as in other socialist systems like China, Yugoslavia, and Vietnam. Even in these states, however, it is worth emphasizing that there are substantial variations in the extent to which these operating authorities are subject to effective supervision on the part of the central government.[24]

The case study of operation included in this volume deals with a situation that is unique as far as the United States is concerned. Since 1910, the federal government has played the role of operating authority in conducting the commercial harvest of northern fur seals on the Pribilof Islands in the central Bering Sea. In effect, this harvest amounts to a nationalized industry currently conducted under the terms of the Fur Seal Act of 1966 (PL 89–702; 80 Stat. 1091, 16 USC 1151 et seq.).[25] It is not even delegated to a public corporation; the harvest is the responsibility of the National Marine Fisheries Service located in the Department of Commerce (prior to 1970 the Bureau of Commercial Fisheries in the Department of the Interior). The work of this operating authority is substantially restricted by the existence of an international regime for northern fur seals set forth in the Interim Convention for the Conservation of Northern Fur Seals of 1957.[26] But nothing in this convention requires the United States to organize the commercial harvest of fur seals as a state monopoly, and the idea of establishing the state as an operating authority to deal with this resource antedates the original fur seal convention of 1911.[27] Accordingly, this case study affords an opportunity to examine a strategy toward the use of natural resources which has been little used in the United States but which some wish to pursue as an interesting option for the future.

REGULATION

It has long been recognized that market failures will occur from time to time, even in an orderly free enterprise, market-oriented system. In fact, the recognition and analysis of market failures constitutes one of the hallmarks of neoclassical microeconomics. There is no reason to expect the realm of natural resources to be unusually free of such problems. Rather, there are excellent grounds for concluding that such failures will be particularly important and pervasive in this realm.[28] These circumstances justify intervention on the part of the state to move the economy as a whole in the direction of allocative efficiency, even when societal decision making about the use of natural resources rests largely in private hands. At least in American practice, however, it is widely held that the state should endeavor to intrude as little as possible in the activities of private actors in the course of correcting for market failures. Thus, regulating an industry is certainly to be preferred to nationalizing it. And in pursuing regulatory strategies, there is a presumption in favor of employing relatively decentralized procedures to alter incentives (for example, charges) in contrast to administrative proscriptions.[29]

No doubt the classic cases of regulation arise under conditions in which some system of private property rights exists but restrictions on competition or spillovers are so pervasive as to justify regulation. This is the origin of the old-line regulatory agencies such as the Interstate Commerce Commission, the Federal Trade Commission, and the Federal Communications Commission, and such problems have certainly given rise to regulatory efforts relating to natural resources (for example, programs to control air and water pollution).[30] At the same time, there is another set of circumstances generating pressures for regulation to correct market failures which are particularly prominent in the realm of natural resources. For one reason or another, it is often hard to articulate or to enforce a suitable structure of private property rights in connection with important natural resources. Well-known cases in point include common pool situations with respect to oil reserves, common property phenomena in the marine fisheries, the nonspecific features of watersheds and airsheds, and the amenities flowing from aesthetically pleasing natural environments.[31] In cases where this problem is severe, it is not enough simply to deploy some standard policy instrument to correct for market failures. Instead, it becomes necessary to institute a system of restricted common property, and this ordinarily gives rise to a role for the state in devising appropriate rules, promulgating the necessary regulations, and obtaining compliance with these regulations.[32] In the United States, the growing stream of forays into the realm of marine resource policy offers numerous examples of this approach to regulation.

The case study of regulation I have selected for this collection deals with the restricted common property regime established under the Fishery Conservation and Management Act of 1976 (PL 94–265; 90 Stat. 331, 16 USC 1801 et seq.).[33] Under the provisions of this Act, the United States claims exclusive management authority over marine fisheries to a distance of 200 miles from the inner boundary of the territorial sea and beyond that point in the case of anadromous species (for example, salmon). No attempt is made to create exclusive private property rights in stocks of fish per se or in specified sections of the fishery conservation zone. Rather, the regime relies upon the development of a structure of rules to guide the behavior of individual fishermen together with a set of organizational arrangements to administer the resultant system. Needless to say, the introduction of this regime has led to the promulgation of many detailed regulations designed to translate the general provisions of the Fishery Conservation and Management Act into a working managerial system. The case study itself focuses on the problems of obtaining compliance on the part of fishermen with these regulations. While this is obviously not the only important issue arising in conjunction with this regime, the issue of compliance has been largely neglected in most of the existing literature on regulation.[34]

Two

The Disposition of Public Lands: The Alaska Native Claims Settlement Act of 1971

Programs designed to transfer public lands and natural resources into private hands have been justified in terms of a variety of social goals during the course of American history. Whether or not these programs have generally proven successful in terms of their stated goals is a controversial matter. But there are good reasons to conclude that they have typically generated unforeseen and unintended consequences of a far-reaching sort. Sometimes these consequences have been valued positively on a more or less widespread basis. More often, however, they have served to illustrate the disruptive potential of policymakers who are poorly informed and limited by institutional constraints, even though it is reasonable to suppose that they mean well. To explore the implications of this proposition, I examine in some depth a case involving the disposition of public lands. In my judgment, this case is representative of a large class of policy problems confronting governments on a regular basis.

THE NATIVE CLAIMS SETTLEMENT ACT

The unresolved claims of the Native peoples of Alaska acquired political prominence in the United States during the 1960s.[1] This is partly attributable to organizational efforts on the part of these peoples, which gave them a growing capacity to advance their claims on a coordinated basis. In part, it is traceable directly to the discovery of extensive reserves of oil and natural gas in Alaska coupled with the realization that the unresolved claims of the Native peoples could pose serious legal impediments to the exploitation of these reserves. The result was a classic episode of legislative bargaining eventuating in the passage of the Alaska Native Claims Settlement Act of 1971 (PL 92–203; 85 Stat. 688, 43 USC 1601 et seq.). From a national point of view, the overriding purpose of this Act was to extinguish all outstanding Native claims to land or compensation arising either from "aboriginal title in Alaska based on use and occupancy" (sec. 4[b]) or from any previous treaties or statutes (sec. 4[c]). In return, however, the Settlement Act provides for the conveyance of formal title to 43.7 million acres of land to the Native peoples in various forms as well as a financial settlement of $962.5 million: $462.5 million to be paid out of general federal funds over a period of eleven years and $500 million to come from royalties, rents, and bonuses accruing from the extraction of minerals or hydrocarbons in the state of Alaska.[2]

To carry out these provisions, the Act outlines an explicit organizational structure, emphasizing the formation of a system of regional corporations coupled with a large collection of village corporations. Without doubt, the Alaska Native regional corporations constitute the key element of the resultant "machinery of settlement."[3] This is so even though the idea of placing primary emphasis on these corporations arose relatively late in the process of negotiating a settlement of the Alaska Native claims,[4] and final agreement on this arrangement emerged from a last-minute compromise between the conferees from the House of Representatives and the Senate.[5] At the same time, it is the subsequent activities of these regional corporations which have led to the most dramatic unforeseen and unintended consequences flowing from the enactment of PL 92–203. In what follows, therefore, I concentrate on an analysis of the activities of the Alaska Native regional corporations during the period since their incorporation during the first six months of 1972.

It is worth emphasizing at the outset that there was nothing inevitable about the creation of a system of regional corporations as the principal organizational innovation of the Native claims settlement. The drive for a claims settlement on the Native side was spearheaded by a statewide organization, the Alaska Federation of Natives (AFN). Draft legislation introduced in Congress in previous years had called for substantially different arrangements with respect to the "machinery of settlement."[6] The Nixon administration's proposals never focused on the idea of establishing regional corporations.[7] Even in 1971, the Senate passed a bill dealing with Alaska Native claims (S. 35) according only a secondary role to the regional corporations and emphasizing instead the role of an Alaska Native Services and Development Corporation and an Alaska Native Investment Corporation.[8] The final system of regional corporations, therefore, constituted an idea that blossomed late in the claims negotiations and triumphed in the complex bargaining processes characteristic of Congressional policymaking.[9]

In principle, there were at least four fundamentally different organizational plans that could have been adopted in conjunction with a settlement of the outstanding Native claims in Alaska. In the first instance, it would have been possible to focus on the individual as the principle claimant and to convey land as well as financial compensation to individual Natives through the medium of loosely organized tribes or other traditional social groupings.[10] In fact, this approach had been adopted on several occasions in prior efforts to settle Indian claims in the "lower forty-eight." But it was widely regarded as a failure because it offered little stimulus for the creation of organizational structures to deal with the social and economic problems of the Native peoples.[11] This approach seems to have had no influential backers in the negotiations leading to the Alaska Native Claims Settlement Act.[12]

Another option would have been to focus on the Native villages of Alaska and to make the village the basic organizational unit of the Native claims settlement. While village Alaska had been in transition for some years before 1971,[13] there can be no doubt that "Most people saw the village as the basic traditional level of Native organization."[14] Such an approach would have emphasized the traditional village way of life even while attempting to set the villages on a firmer economic footing and to alleviate the extreme problems of health, education, and welfare characteristic of village Alaska in the presettlement period.[15] Major doubts concerning this option centered on the extreme volatility of many Native villages and the problems of stabilizing these communities sufficiently to serve as the key to the organizational structure of the claims settlement.

The option of creating a system of regional corporations was pushed by those calling for a "modern settlement." The premise underlying this approach was "that the village way of life was dying and that the new Native was interested more in economic development than in the traditional life of the village."[16] Under the circumstances, the Native peoples should be encouraged to participate increasingly in the cash economy and to operate in the world of business with profit maximization as a major objective. Both the innovative character and the size of the regional corporations were seen as fostering the development of this orientation. While this approach appealed to certain members of the Native population, it also attracted many nonNatives who perceived it as a method of stimulating private economic development and creating large-scale business enterprises throughout the state of Alaska.[17]

A final option would have placed primary emphasis on

one or more statewide organizations. This might have taken the form of expanding the role of the AFN or some successor organization. Alternatively, it might have involved creating an Alaska Native Development Corporation as called for in the bill transmitted to Congress by the administration in 1971 (H.R. 7432) or some combination of statewide organizations such as those outlined in the Senate bill (S. 35). For some, an attraction of this approach lay in its inevitably making the Native peoples as a group a powerful force in the state politics of Alaska. For others, the same prospect constituted the major drawback of this approach. Thus, the report of the House Committee on Interior and Insular Affairs stated explicitly that the ''corporate organizations provided for in the bill are intended to avoid the creation of one or more giant corporate entities, based on ethnic origin, that might become in effect the third level of government in the State.''[18]

The specific system of regional corporations outlined in PL 92-203 incorporates features that require at least brief notice in this discussion. For purposes of the claims settlement the Act divides the state of Alaska into twelve geographical regions (sec. 7[a]). Each of these regions is to have a single regional corporation whose members or shareholders are to be the Native peoples residing in that geographical region or claiming the region as their place of origin.[19] In addition, the Act provides for the creation of a thirteenth regional corporation to be composed of Natives who are no longer resident in Alaska (sec. 7[c]). Individual Natives born before 18 December 1971 automatically become stockholders in one of these regional corporations with each person receiving 100 shares of common stock in the appropriate corporation (sec. 7[g]).[20] The actual number of shareholders in these regional corporations varies considerably from a high of more than fifteen thousand in the case of Sealaska Corporation to a low of just over one thousand in the case of Ahtna, Inc. Table 1 indicates the distribution of membership in the regional corporations.

TABLE 1
MEMBERSHIP IN THE REGIONAL CORPORATIONS

Corporation	Number of stock- holders (9-14-74)	Stock- holders residing in region (8-28-74)	Total population within region (1970)	Number of village corpora- tions	Number of stock- holders (12-31-77)
Ahtna, Inc.	1,092	495	1,332	8	1,057
Aleut Corporation	3,353	1,667	7,694	12	3,124
Arctic Slope Regional Corp.	3,906	2,886	3,266	8	3,710
Bering Straits Native Corp.	6,916	4,638	5,749	16	6,271
Bristol Bay Native Corp.	5,517	3,596	4,995	29	5,315
Calista Corp.	13,441	11,561	12,617	56	13,193
Chugach Natives, Inc.	2,099	1,062	6,286	5	1,881
Cook Inlet Region, Inc.	6,243	4,181	145,072	6	6,052
Doyon, Ltd.	9,221	6,683	57,354	34	8,905
Koniag, Inc.	3,340	1,958	9,409	9	3,267
NANA	4,905	3,643	4,043	11	4,755
Sealaska Corp.	16,493	9,529	42,565	9	15,388
Thirteenth Region	—	—	—	—	4,005
Totals	76,526	51,899	300,382	203	76,923

NOTE: Most of the changes between 1974 and 1976 are the result of the court-ordered election held in 1976 for the thirteenth region.

SOURCES: (i) Enrollment data: Enrollment Office, U.S. Bureau of Indian Affairs, Anchorage, Alaska, and *Annual Report on the Implementation of the Alaska Native Claims Settlement Act, As Amended,* As Required by sec. 23 of PL 92–203, January 1, 1977–December 31, 1977, (ii) Population: U.S. Bureau of the Census, U.S. Census of Population, 1970, Alaska.

All of the financial compensation called for under the terms of the Act is to be funneled through an entity called the Alaska Native Fund established in the United States Treasury (sec. 6[a]). Initially, all this money is to be transmitted to the regional corporations and divided among them on the basis of number of shareholders (sec. 6[c]). During the first five years of the settlement, the regional corporations are to dispose of the money as follows: 10 percent to regional stockholders, 45 percent to village corporations and region at-large stockholders, [21] and 45 percent to the regional corporations themselves. Thereafter, the regional corporations are to use the following rule of division: 50 percent to the village corporations and region at-large stockholders and 50 percent to the regional corporations themselves (sec. 7[j]). As mentioned previously, the $462.5 million from general federal funds is to be paid out over eleven years ending in 1982. The payout schedule for the remaining $500 million is harder to specify since it depends on the rate of mineral extraction in Alaska, but the final payment is expected to occur by the end of 1991.[22] Under the circumstances, the basic operating capital of the regional corporations is relatively large (something over $400 million), but it is finite and not replenishable from external sources.[23]

With respect to the land settlement, it is necessary to draw a clear distinction between surface rights and the subsurface estate. The village corporations rather than the regional corporations are identified in PL 92-203 as the primary recipients of the surface rights to land conveyed to the Native peoples (secs. 11 and 12). Nevertheless, six regional corporations are designated as recipients of surface rights to 16 million acres under a "land-loss" formula designed to compensate the legitimate claims of several groups of Natives whose historic rights to the land would not be accurately reflected in calculations based strictly on current population.[24] In addition, the regional corporations are ultimately to receive title to the surface rights to a large fraction of 2 million acres set aside under the Act for special purposes. Figure 1 summarizes the distribution of surface rights called for under the terms of the Native Claims Settlement Act. The situation with regard to the subsurface estate is entirely different. All of the subsurface rights to the Alaska Native lands go to the twelve local regional corporations with

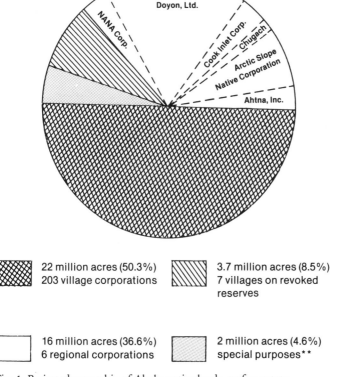

22 million acres (50.3%) 203 village corporations		3.7 million acres (8.5%) 7 villages on revoked reserves	
16 million acres (36.6%) 6 regional corporations		2 million acres (4.6%) special purposes**	

Fig. 1. Projected ownership of Alaska native lands, surface estate.

**Special purposes category includes one township to each special named city (Juneau, Sitka, Kodiak, and Kenai); allotments; Alaska native groups; and land designated as cemeteries and historic sites which goes to each of the twelve regional corporations. After these special purposes are met, the remainder will be divided among the twelve corporations.

Source: Land Distribution Chart, "Alaska Native Management Report," 31 March 1975

the exception of certain small areas falling under the heading
of special purposes and of 3.7 million acres owned by certain
villages that were once in reservations and that have opted
not to participate in the system of regional corporations.[25]
What this means is that the regional corporations occupy a
dominant position under the terms of the claims settlement
with respect to the extraction of oil, natural gas, and hard
minerals on Alaska Native lands.[26] Figure 2 summarizes the
division of the subsurface estate of the Alaska Native lands
among the regional corporations.

The regional corporations are to be normal profit-

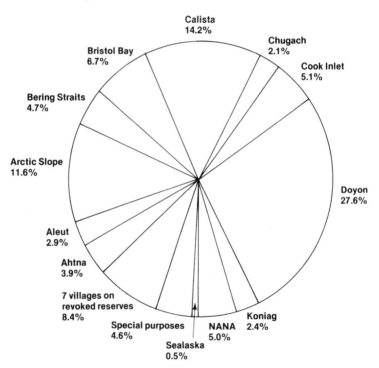

Fig. 2. Projected ownership of Alaska native lands, subsurface estate. Twelve
regional corporations will hold title to the subsurface estate of each special
city, Alaska native groups, cemeteries, and historic sites. Title to the
subsurface estate of allotments will be held by the federal government.
Percent divisions are based upon Land Distribution Chart, "Alaska Native
Management Report," 31 March 1975.

making business enterprises incorporated under Alaska law. In fact, however, there appears to have been some disagreement concerning appropriate guidelines for the operation of these corporations. The Senate report (accompanying S. 35) states that "The land claims settlement bill approved by the Committee offers the Natives of Alaska a real opportunity to break the chain of poverty which circumscribes their lives from birth, to bring needed services and public works to their home communities and to develop their human and natural resources."[27] And it appears to suggest that the regional corporations might play a major role in pursuing these objectives.[28] The conference committee reports, in contrast, observe that "the conference committee has adopted a policy of self-determination on the part of the Alaska Native people" and further that the "conference committee also contemplates that the Regional and Village Corporations will not expend funds for purposes other than those reasonably necessary in the course of ordinary business operations."[29] The Act itself states only that the regional corporations "shall incorporate under the laws of Alaska . . . to conduct business for profit" (sec. 7[d]). As we shall see in later sections of this chapter, the resultant ambiguity has led to several serious problems in the implementation of the Native claims settlement.

The Act is quite specific, however, in setting forth several special features that the regional corporations are to exhibit. In the first instance, shares of stock in the corporations are to be inalienable for a period of twenty years (sec. 7[h]). That is, there are to be no transfers of stock in these corporations, except through inheritance, until 1992 (though the corporations themselves are free to buy and sell land). Next, the land belonging to the corporations is to be exempt from real property taxes through 1991, unless it is developed or leased for profit (sec. 21[d]). Moreover, the corporations are required to engage in a relatively complicated revenue-sharing plan among themselves. Specifically, section 7[i] requires that "Seventy per centum of all revenues received by each Regional Corporation from the timber resources and subsurface estate patented to it pursuant to this Act shall be divided annually by the Regional Corporation among all twelve Regional Corporations organized pursuant to this section according to the number of Natives enrolled in each region.'' In recent years, this rather imprecise provision has given rise to extensive controversy and has now become a serious bone of contention among different groups of Alaska Natives.[30]

The other major element of the "machinery of settlement" called for under PL 92–203 is a collection of village corporations (sec. 8).[31] In the period since the passage of the Act a total of 246 village corporations "have been formed to receive land and benefits as provided by the Settlement Act."[32] As of 1978, there were 191 separate village corporations.[33] The difference in these figures can be explained: some of these corporations have been declared ineligible[34] and others have merged either with each other or with the regional corporation for their area.[35] The exact relationship between the regional corporations and the village corporations is a matter of considerable uncertainty. It has given rise to a series of complex legal issues, many of which remain unresolved at this time. Nevertheless, it is clear that the power of the regional corporations is overwhelming compared to that of even the larger village corporations.[36] All of the money going to the village corporations passes through regional corporations that have some control over the conditions under which these funds are to be disbursed.[37] The resources of the regional corporations are far greater than those of the village corporations.[38] The regional corporations are not only financially dominant, they are also a magnet for the outstanding leadership talent in the Native community. Under the circumstances, the village corporations often find themselves applying to the regional corporations for help, and the regional corporations typically dominate joint ventures between village corporations and regional corporations. Moreover, the Act includes several specific provisions that have the effect of solidifying the dominant position of the regional corporations (sec. 8). For example, the initial articles of incorporation for the villages were subject to approval by the regional corporations. Similarly, "Amendments to the articles of incorporation and the annual budgets of the Village Corporations shall, for a period of five years, be subject to review and approval by the Regional Corporation" (sec. 8[b]).[39]

The dominant position of the regional corporations is further enhanced because PL 92-203 (unlike S. 35) does not call for any statewide organizations among the Native peoples and contains no provisions for nonprofit enterprises to address problems of welfare and social services.[40] The regional corporations constitute the most comprehensive Native organizations sanctioned by the Settlement Act.[41] The AFN remains in existence and continues to play a relatively active role in Native affairs. But the AFN is dependent upon the regional corporations for financial support. Thus, an agreement was struck toward the end of 1973 under which each regional corporation is to "contribute $8,000 plus $1 for each of its members annually toward the cost of operating the AFN."[42] Similarly, a variety of nonprofit organizations have sprung up at both state and regional levels to take steps toward alleviating pressing problems of health, education, and welfare among the Native peoples of Alaska.[43] But these organizations are dependent upon increasingly scarce grants and volunteer labor; they are pale operations by comparison with the corporate strength of the regional corporations. All in all, the organizational dominance of the regional corporations is striking, and it seems entirely appropriate to focus on their activities in this inquiry into the unforeseen and unintended consequences of the Native Claims Settlement Act.

ECONOMIC PERFORMANCE

Given the fact that PL 92-203 requires that the regional corporations be established as profit-making business enterprises, it is pertinent to start with a brief account of their

economic performance before going on to investigate the
unforeseen and unintended consequences of their activities.
Not surprisingly, there is great variation among the regional
corporations, and it is not easy to generalize about their economic performance. As the discussion in the previous section
suggests, the regional corporations cover a wide spectrum
with respect to such matters as membership, capital, and
control over land.[44] In addition, there is good reason to conclude that the natural resources under the control of the
regional corporations are distributed unevenly. There are
great variations in the sociocultural characteristics of the
various regions. And in the years since 1972, the regional corporations have exhibited considerable differences in the
evolution of their investment philosophies and strategies.
Nevertheless, it is possible to formulate some general conclusions about the economic performance of these enterprises.[45]

Above all, each of the regional corporations has been
forced to choose between placing primary emphasis on programs aimed at stabilizing village Alaska on some new economic foundation or on a strategy of pursuing profit maximization largely through the acquisition of investment properties
unsuitable for decentralized operation in rural areas.[46] The
stabilization of village Alaska would require large expenditures on various forms of social overhead and employment
programs, an orientation more characteristic of public agencies with taxing power than of profit-making business enterprises. In contrast, profit maximization requires a deliberate
policy of directing few resources toward rural areas, thereby
minimizing the effectiveness of the regional corporations in
contributing to improvements in the day-to-day quality of
life of the majority of the Native peoples. The pressures
toward tilting in the direction of profit maximization have
been strong, and it seems accurate to say that most of the
regional corporations have shown a marked tendency to move
in this direction in the years since their incorporation. There
are, however, some exceptions to this generalization. For
example, NANA has placed considerable emphasis on the

development of industries (e.g. reindeer herding) suitable for rural areas, and several of the other regional corporations have shown a real sensitivity toward the needs of the village communities. Thus, it is probably accurate to interpret the recent internal controversy within Sealaska, at least in part, as a conflict over this basic question of priorities.[47]

Other questions of investment strategy facing the regional corporations concern such things as attitudes toward risk and the relative emphasis to be placed on economic growth versus income-producing ventures. There are inherent pressures toward a conservative posture with respect to risk arising because the resources available to the regional corporations constitute the bulk of the patrimony of the Native peoples. If these resources are lost or squandered, there is no reason to suppose that new claims can be raised to be traded away for compensation from the federal government.[48] Under the circumstances, it is somewhat surprising to observe that several of the regional corporations (e.g. Calista, Bering Straits) have engaged in some high risk ventures and paid a high price for doing so. Presumably, the desire to pursue large gains as a profit-making business enterprise triumphed in these cases over the forces of conservatism arising from the role of trustee for the people's patrimony. On the question of growth versus the generation of income, there is again a complex mixture of incentives. Economic growth is attractive to those who focus on the expectation that the flow of external capital to the corporations will decline and become more unpredictable after 1982 and that the tax exemptions set forth in the Act will expire after 1991. But the generation of income over the short-term future seems critical to those who are primarily concerned with the extreme problems of social welfare in village Alaska and with the need to stabilize the rural economy of areas heavily populated by Native peoples. All of these pressures are strong, and it is hard to detect any uniform pattern in the investment decisions of the regional corporations with respect to this broad issue.

Quite apart from the question of goals, all of the regional corporations have run into severe problems in formulating and pursuing economic strategies. In the first instance, they have all experienced a need for extensive and costly legal services.[49] One close observer has pointed out that "Legal costs alone have easily exceeded 10% of the ANCSA Settlement funds paid to the corporations by the spring of 1977."[50] Each of the regional corporations has had to contend with the relative scarcity of Native personnel with talent and experience in the realm of large-scale business activities. Though this is hardly the fault of the Native peoples, it has led to severe problems in some instances. Several of the regional corporations (e.g. Aleut) have had painful and costly experiences with outsiders hired in the early years to provide business knowledge and acumen. Others (e.g. Bering Straits) have run into serious problems arising from the financial decisions of inexperienced Native officers and boards of directors. Beyond this, the corporations have suffered from an understandable tendency toward "patrimonialism" or the making of decisions on the basis of personal or family ties rather than hardheaded business calculation.[51] While it is hard to attach numbers to patrimonialism, the impact of its various forms is widely thought to have been substantial since 1972. Finally, the regional corporations have had to struggle with the scarcity and riskiness of investment opportunities in rural areas alluded to previously.[52] The absence of large, affluent markets, the lack of socioeconomic infrastructure in rural areas, and the volatility of many industries characteristic of rural areas (e.g. commercial fishing) all contribute to the scarcity of rural investment opportunities. Under the circumstances, the regional corporations have been forced to turn their attention toward urban investments to operate as successful profit-making enterprises even though the real expertise of most Natives lies in the realm of rural activities rather than urban industries.

Given all these problems coupled with the requirement of a running-in period for new businesses before they become profitable, it is not particularly surprising that the record of most of the regional corporations in terms of standard economic indicators is rather poor. While they do not tell the entire story, the figures presented in table 2 are clearly indicative of the problems of the regional corporations in purely economic terms. Few of the regional corporations have shown a positive return per share on any sustained basis. This means not only that they have generally been unable to contribute directly to the economic welfare of their stockholders but also that they have not had extensive profits to reinvest in the continued expansion of the business.[53] In addition, several of the corporations are heavily indebted, and some of them have not exhibited much vigor in the employment of assets to generate gross income. To date, the most successful regional corporations in economic terms appear to be Ahtna, Inc. and Doyon, Ltd. Ahtna is the smallest of the regional corporations and has had the good fortune of benefiting from particularly careful management. For its part, Doyon has extensive land holdings and has benefited from the exploitation of natural resources in its region.[54] NANA constitutes another interesting case since it has succeeded in making a profit even while placing considerable emphasis on the development of new employment opportunities in rural areas. Again in economic terms, the most serious failures have been suffered by Bering Straits and Arctic Slope. Bering Straits has made a series of unfortunate investments and now faces a severe financial crisis involving, among other things, growing unrest among its creditors. Arctic Slope, by contrast, has expended substantial resources on various policy issues (e.g. the bowhead whale controversy) but is nevertheless widely regarded as secure because it probably possesses extensive reserves of oil and natural gas.[55]

While the economic problems of the regional corporations are not particularly surprising, they are certainly serious. Any business venture that has not achieved financial stability after five to six years is on somewhat shaky ground. Investment opportunities in Alaska are not especially attractive for new and insecure corporations. This is partly because of the

TABLE 2
REGIONAL CORPORATION FINANCES

Corporation	Shares outstanding	Debt ratio	Asset turnover	Return on assets	Return (loss) per share
Ahtna, Inc.					
1975	105,900	.23	.32	.11	$1.91
1976	105,900	.43	.16	.02	.60
1977	105,900	.42	.38	.02	.58
Aleut Corporation					
1975	336,200	.32	.06	-	($1.06)
1976	306,400	.47	.20	-	(2.29)
1977	306,400	.60	-	-	(1.45)
Arctic Slope Regional Corp.					
1975	391,000	.29	.22	-	($1.95)
1976	379,700	.46	.29	-	(6.36)
Bering Straits Native Corp.					
1975	555,600	.15	.11	-	($ .62)
1976	555,600	.84	.56	-	(8.22)
Bristol Bay Native Corp.					
1975	528,000	.05	.14	.01	$ .11
1976	528,000	.68	.33	-	(1.58)
1977	528,000	.55	1.27	.10	5.71
Calista Corp.					
1975	1,345,500	.09	.07	-	($1.69)
1976	1,326,500	.25	.06	-	(2.57)
1977	1,319,700	.57	.19	-	(1.71)
Chugach Natives, Inc.					
1975	187,200	.30	.56	nil	$ .01
1976	187,200	.35	.44	-	(2.26)
1977	187,000	.31	.20	-	(2.37)
Cook Inlet Region, Inc.					
1975	627,300	.48	.15	.01	$ .41
1976	599,400	.50	.16	-	(.84)

TABLE 2 *(cont.)*

Corporation	Shares outstanding	Debt ratio	Asset turnover	Return on assets	Return (loss) per share
Doyon, Ltd.					
1975	924,600	.10	.10	.01	$ .23
1976	880,500	.09	.16	.05	1.08
Koniag, Inc.					
1975	334,000	.25	.11	-	($ .87)
1976	312,100	.35	.15	-	(2.32)
1977	326,800	.34	.28	-	(1.30)
NANA					
1975	725,200	.43	.44	.03	$ .66
1976	725,200	.55	.99	nil	.01
Sealaska Corp.					
1975	1,634,000	.02	.08	.01	$ .09
1976	1,495,416	.01	.05	-	(.04)
1977	1,497,756	.23	.31	.01	.29

NOTES:
  Definition of ratios:
    Debt ratio = $\dfrac{\text{total debt}}{\text{total assets}}$

    Asset turnover = $\dfrac{\text{gross income}}{\text{total assets}}$

    Return on assets = $\dfrac{\text{net income}}{\text{total assets}}$

    Return (loss) per share = $\dfrac{\text{net income (loss)}}{\text{shares outstanding}}$

The debt ratio shows the extent to which management has used debt capital to finance asset acquisitions. A debt ratio of 0.50, for example, indicates that one-half of asset book values are financed by debt capital.

The asset turnover ratio suggests how actively management has employed assets to generate gross income. Only one corporation has managed to use a dollar of assets to generate more than a dollar of gross income—but this corporation had large extraordinary entries for that year.

The net return on assets ratio reflects management's success at

TABLE 2 *(cont.)*

preserving asset productivity through effective cost control. High
levels of gross income can be lost through ineffective management
of direct and indirect costs.

Return per share outstanding is the basic measure of corporate
financial performance. If ANCSA shares were marketable, it would
be this measure that most analysts would compute in their effort to
price the shares of a given corporation.

SOURCE: Dean F. Olson, ''A 3-Year Financial Analysis of ANCSA
Regional Corporations,'' *Alaska Native Management Report* 6 (1
December 1977): 4–7.

problems of investment in rural areas mentioned previously.
But even in the realm of the vast potential wealth associated
with Alaska's natural resources there are problems. The
capital required to exploit these resources typically is enor-
mous, and the risks are often so great that even the giants of
the oil industry tend to form consortia in this area to spread
the risk.[56] Moreover, the regional corporations must look
forward to the time in the not-too-distant future when they
will have to stand on their own financially and relinquish
their current tax advantages. The annual injection of federal
funds terminates in 1982, and all of the funds arising from
the settlement are expected to be distributed by 1992. The
lands owned by the corporations will become subject to state
and local real property taxes at the same time (sec. 21[d]).
Consequently, the pressure on the regional corporations to
achieve financial stability over the next few years is great.
They face an approaching situation in which operating costs
will increase and the flow of external funds will cease more or
less simultaneously.

DE FACTO CONSEQUENCES

Turning from the issue of economic performance, let us
explore a range of de facto consequences of the activities of
the regional corporations which were largely unforeseen and

unintended when PL 92–203 was signed on 18 December 1971. It is increasingly fashionable in certain quarters to blame the disruption of village Alaska and the impairment of cultural integrity among the Native peoples of Alaska on the organizational structure promulgated by the Settlement Act. But such sweeping generalizations are surely unfounded.

In the years before the passage of PL 92–203, the Native communities of Alaska were beset by a wide range of socioeconomic ills.[57] The average age at death among Natives in 1966 was 34.5 years. Native populations experienced an incidence of major diseases, infant mortality, alcoholism, and suicide far in excess of nonNative populations in Alaska. The overwhelming majority of Native housing was substandard and unsanitary. And extreme poverty was an almost uniform way of life among Native peoples. Thus, a 1971 report states that "Village family income for those who have any income averages less than one-quarter of the family income for non-Native Alaskans."[58] In short, life in village Alaska at the time of the settlement was nasty and short, whether or not it was unusually brutish. That many of these conditions are traceable in one way or another to encounters between the Natives and white populations of Russia and America over a period of several hundred years does nothing to alter the facts of the situation. Laudatory comments referring to the traditional Native way of life and to the cultural integrity of the Native peoples of Alaska are certainly not descriptive of any conditions obtaining during the recent past.

Nor is it accurate to argue that the communities of village Alaska were stable or viable during the period before the passage of the Settlement Act.[59] On the contrary, these communities had been undergoing a variety of dramatic changes for some time before 1971.[60] On the demographic front, these changes included: a rapid growth of total Native population, the consolidation of villages coupled with the abandonment of smaller communities, a dramatic migration of Natives to the cities, and the development of numerous links between the villages and the cities.[61] Concomitant economic and technological changes took the following forms: the spread of the cash economy, the rapid introduction of specific new technologies (e.g. rifles, steel traps, gasoline engines, snowmobiles, metal boats), and the capital intensification of subsistence hunting and gathering.[62] And all these changes gave rise to a variety of sociocultural developments such as: a rapid growth of new desires and felt needs, the rise of intergenerational conflict, and the decline of traditional authority structures.[63] In short, the communities of village Alaska were already in the midst of disruptive transformation by 1971, and there can be no doubt that the human costs of this transitional situation would have been high regardless of the approach to the settlement of Native claims arrived at through the legislative process.[64]

It follows that it is not reasonable to blame the problems afflicting the Native peoples of Alaska on the regional corporations created under the terms of PL 92–203. Nevertheless, the establishment of these corporations as the principal organizational vehicle of the claims settlement has led to a variety of important unforeseen and unintended consequences. These consequences have intensified the disruptive forces at work in village Alaska and they have served to impede or prevent initiatives that might have been pursued in an effort to stabilize the Native communities of Alaska on some new foundation. It is possible to identify and to differentiate among a range of these consequences arising from the activities of the regional corporations during the years since their incorporation in 1972.

Day-to-Day Life

The direct impact of the regional corporations on the day-to-day existence of most individual Natives has been minimal. Payments to individuals from the Alaska Native Fund during the first five years of the settlement, channeled through the regional corporations, ''were disappointingly small'' averaging ''approximately $410 to Natives enrolled in village corporations and approximately $2,250 to those signed up 'at large.' ''[65] Dividends from the regional corporations have been nil or negligible. By 1978, only Ahtna and Arctic Slope had paid any dividends at all.[66] With respect to subsistence activities, the creation of the corporations has had little impact so far. A large proportion of the land used for subsistence hunting and gathering will not in the end belong to the Natives. Instead, subsistence use will presumably be given priority treatment on many public lands in Alaska.[67] Where the relevant land has been selected by Native groups, it has not yet been subjected to significant development so that subsistence use remains largely unhindered.[68] And of course, eventual economic development affecting such lands can only have the effect of complicating subsistence activities. Beyond this, the regional corporations have done little to ease the problems of the Native peoples in the realms of health, welfare, and social services. Though the regional corporations have not been totally insensitive to these problems, they have tended to emphasize more straightforward business ventures, leaving social and welfare programs to an array of nonprofit organizations. Consequently, few alterations in the quality of life for ordinary Natives are attributable to the activities of the regional corporations. Finally, there is little scope for the average Native to participate in the decision making of his regional corporation or to acquire a sense of active participatoin in any other way.[69] This is the result of several factors including: lack of understanding of corporate practices, distance from corporate headquarters, inability to attend stockholders' meetings, or residence outside the region altogether.[70] Under the circumstances, the regional corporation typically becomes a distant entity whose activities are only dimly perceived and poorly understood by residents of the Native communities.[71]

This situation has led to numerous misunderstandings on the part of individual Natives concerning the nature and function of the regional corporations.[72] Even worse, it has generated disturbing levels of apathy, alienation, and anger among many Natives. Some of the regional corporations report difficulty in inducing shareholders to participate even to the extent of casting proxy ballots or to maintain simple records of stock changing hands through inheritance. Disappointed expectations are widespread in the Native communities. And anger or negative feelings directed toward the officers of the regional corporations are not uncommon. For example, there are cases in which Natives running for elective office in the state find it prudent to deemphasize their association with a regional corporation to avoid losing favor among their Native constituents. In short, the regional corporations have not become popular among the rank-and-file, however one evaluates their performance in other terms.

Health, Education, and Welfare

As mentioned previously, the overwhelming immediate needs of the Native peoples of Alaska lie in the following areas: health, housing, education, employment opportunities, and the maintenance of cultural integrity.[73] This general point has been documented many times, perhaps most dramatically in the massive report entitled *Alaska Natives and the Land* completed in 1968.[74] Yet, the regional corporations have done little to alleviate these problems and in some instances they have ignored them completely. This is partly attributable to the establishment of the regional corporations as profit-making enterprises that were instructed to spend money for ordinary business operations. In part, it stems from a desire not to give federal or state officials any excuse to terminate or reduce public welfare programs directed toward the Native peoples of Alaska.[75] This is not to say that those making decisions for the regional corporations are totally insensitive to the welfare and social service needs of the Native peoples.[76] But there is no doubt that the "machinery of settlement" outlined in the Settlement Act operates to

impede concerted and well-funded efforts to improve the
quality of life prevailing in the Native communities.

In fact, a variety of nonprofit organizations has emerged
since 1971 to spearhead efforts to meet these needs in the
realms of welfare and social services. They include the Alaska
Native Foundation at the state level as well as numerous
regional organizations specializing in such areas as health,
housing, and cultural matters. But the situation of these
nonprofit organizations is precarious at best. Thus, ''They are
funded solely through whatever state, federal or private
grants they can scare up and often the money allowed is too
little to meet Alaska's high cost of living and travel.''[77] Grant
funds are never abundant, and there is some tendency for
potential grantors to be deterred by the presence of the
''rich'' regional corporations that could contribute more
toward the search for solutions to the welfare and social service problems of the Native peoples. Moreover, ''Because
financial backing is inadequate and unstable, the non-profits
are seldom able to attract and hold top quality management.''[78] In short, while PL 92–203 does not formally bar the
creation of organizations oriented toward the overwhelming
immediate needs of the Native peoples, it has had the effect
of making it painfully difficult to deal with these needs in a
forceful manner.

Economic Development

As mentioned previously, the regional corporations will
experience growing pressure to generate liquid capital on
their own during the foreseeable future. As the flow of funds
through the Alaska Native Fund comes to an end and the tax
exemptions of the Settlement Act are removed after 1991, the
need to raise additional capital assets will become pressing.[79]
This need may be met in part by income from investments in
urban properties and commercial ventures. But the record of
the regional corporations so far suggests that these sources of
funds are not likely to be sufficient to meet the financial

requirements of the corporations after 1991. Under the circumstances, two other sources of revenue will become increasingly attractive. After 1991, a market in shares of stock in these corporations may emerge (sec. 7[h][3]). Even if the corporations are not performing well in terms of conventional economic indicators, the potential value of their nonliquid assets may give their stock substantial market value. But this could lead to a situation in which the Native corporations begin to lose their character as Native enterprises, and there is likely to be powerful resistance to the strategy of exploiting this source of liquid capital.[80] The obvious alternative will be for the corporations themselves to exploit the subsurface mineral wealth of their regions or to sell land (or rights) to nonNative interests.[81] Already, several of the regional corporations have entered into agreements with major oil companies or other firms interested in the natural resources of the Native areas of Alaska.[82] And there is every reason to expect that the resource potential of these areas coupled with the pressure on the regional corporations to generate liquid capital will lead to extensive economic development in the Native areas over the next twenty years.

The consequences of this sequence of events, however, will inevitably raise several major problems. Economic development in the Native areas will provoke opposition among environmentalists anxious to preserve large natural environments in Alaska and lead to further conflicts between the Natives and environmentalists like the current controversy over the bowhead whale.[83] The exploitation of timber and mineral resources will conflict with the continued pursuit of subsistence hunting and gathering in some areas. This will have the unfortunate effect of exacerbating conflicts among the Natives themselves and of stimulating additional displeasure with the regional corporations on the part of Natives living in rural communities. Above all, extensive economic development will call into question some of the most deep-seated, traditional Native attitudes toward the land and natural environments. For example, it is hard to square large-scale mining operations with the traditional Native desire to live in harmony with nature.[84] Increasingly, this prospect is a source of concern and distress among thoughtful and articulate Natives. But the pressure on the regional corporations to generate liquid capital will be great, and the Settlement Act grants the regional corporations extensive legal authority over the natural resources of the Native areas.

"Brain Drain"

The creation of the regional corporation produced an immediate need for a large number of capable individuals to occupy executive positions. Moreover, the magnitude of the resources available to the regional corporations gave them a decisive advantage over other Native organizations in the competition for talented individuals. But the pool of talented and trained Natives was (and in fact remains) small; there simply were not enough capable individuals to go around. The inevitable result of this situation was an impoverishment of the villages and rural communities in terms of human resources.[85] Thus, the villages, which had traditionally been the primary form of organization among the Native peoples, quickly lost many of their most promising leaders and were left to confront the disruptive forces described previously with few younger and more vigorous leaders. Those who left to take over the new regional corporations were typically the younger males who had received at least some education at Bureau of Indian Affairs (BIA) or state schools outside their native villages.[86] Under the circumstances, the emergence of the regional corporations has led to the development of a two-class system among the Natives. On the one hand, there are the younger executives of the regional corporations who are increasingly urbanized and who are derisively described as "Brooks Brothers Natives" by their critics.[87] On the other hand, there are the older rural leaders who continue to struggle to maintain traditional ways but who are ill prepared to cope with the management of the new village corporations created under the terms of the Settlement Act. And the problems of communication and understanding between the two groups are severe despite the commendable efforts of organizations like the Alaska Federation of Natives to find ways to bridge the gap.[88]

Urban/Rural Integration

For some time, the remoteness and sense of isolation of village Alaska has been declining.[89] This is partly a consequence of the introduction of modern forms of communication and transportation. In part, it is a result of the continuing flow of Natives from rural communities to the cities.[90] But there can be little doubt that the emergence of the regional corporations has expanded and accelerated this process of integration. There is now a class of highly mobile Native executives who move freely about the state of Alaska, make regular trips to Washington on business, and generally spread a wide range of new interests and expectations among the Native peoples of Alaska. The business ventures of the regional corporations have not only brought new commercial activities to some rural areas, they have also brought numerous individual Natives to the cities for training or to work in Native-owned enterprises.[91] Further, the regional corporations have attempted to encourage shareholders to take an interest in corporate affairs and in some instances even to travel to urban centers for such things as stockholders' meetings. Of course, none of these developments is surprising in conjunction with the pursuit of large-scale business ventures. But they have had the effect of intensifying the disruptive forces affecting village Alaska and heightening the widespread sense of uncertainty and confusion concerning the social and cultural identity of the Native peoples. The result is a growing sense of unease within the Native community. Numerous forces, including the activities of the regional corporations, are pushing the Natives toward the social patterns of the white world. Yet there are many who sympathize with the following sentiments expressed by the authors of *Letters to Howard*: "We don't want to become better white men or beat them at their own game. We just want a chance to develop our traditional values into a satisfying way of life that we can understand. AN ACT is forcing us into new ways of organizing ourselves and doing things before we really understand what is happening."[92]

Decline of Village Life

While there is no doubt that village Alaska was experiencing the impact of disruptive forces at the time of the Settlement Act in 1971, there is also general agreement that the village had been the primary organizational unit of the Native peoples over a long period of time.[93] At the same time, there is considerable truth to the charge that the villages and their corporations are the stepchildren of the Settlement Act. The problems of the villages under the organizational structure set forth in PL 92-203 are massive. "In general, villages lack: a) qualified Native management experts in the villages; b) the financial resources to hire outside expertise and c) adequate service structures to facilitate receiving outside assistance, such as reliable telephone service, inexpensive transportation, etc."[94] The subsurface estate of each village is controlled by the regional corporation. The regional corporations tend to dominate joint ventures between themselves and the village corporations, and the cash flowing to many villages from the Alaska Native Fund is insufficient even to cover basic operating expenses.[95] As a result, the economic position of many villages is marginal, and serious economic crises are inevitable at the village level during the foreseeable future.[96] As one recent report puts it, "If local corporations do not get help . . . all villages under 600 in population probably do not have revenues sufficient to even hire staff to evaluate business decisions or implement good management practices. In fact, a recent survey shows

that 78 Village Corporations are on the Alaska State Department of Commerce Corporate Violation list, and that twelve
have even been dissolved.''[97]

The point of this discussion is that the last-minute legislative decision to focus on the regional corporations as the key
element of the ''machinery of settlement'' has served to bar
the search for and implementation of creative responses to
the massive problems of village Alaska.[98] Not only are the
regional corporations in a dominant position with respect to
the resources allocated by the Act, their organizational characteristics and requirements also compel a redirection of
attention away from the villages. Yet, the villages remain the
principal site of Native problems in Alaska. Despite the
migration of Natives to the major cities, approximately 70
percent of the Native peoples continue to live in village
Alaska.[99] Though there has been some improvement in indicators of health, education, and welfare since 1968, the
quality of life in the villages and rural communities still leaves
much to be desired. And the villages offer the most dramatic
examples of cultural confusion and disruption among the
Native peoples. Under the circumstances, it is hardly surprising that many observers have noted a striking rise in anomie,
internal conflict, and harsh resentment toward whites over
the same period during which the Natives have been receiving the ''benefits'' of the generous settlement outlined in PL
92–203. There is a grave danger, therefore, that the Native
claims settlement will come to be seen as a tragic failure,
regardless of the extent to which the regional corporations
succeed or fail in conventional economic terms.

It is hard to escape the conclusion that these unforeseen
and unintended consequences of the Settlement Act are of
fundamental importance. In the long run, they may well
generate or contribute to intangible disruptions whose costs
outweigh the more tangible benefits flowing from the Act.
Of course, it may be said that the intent of Congress was to
ensure the achievement of ''self-determination on the part of

the Alaska Native people"[100] and to avoid the charges of paternalism associated with past efforts to deal with the problems of native peoples. Consequently, the remaining difficulties of the Alaska Natives are largely the concern of the Native peoples themselves and not to be treated as the responsibility of any public agency in the wake of the settlement outlined in PL 92–203. But this argument is unpersuasive. To the extent that both continuing and new problems facing the Native peoples of Alaska are traceable to the organizational structure laid down in the Settlement Act, Congress cannot escape responsibility for the ensuing situation. If the basic argument of this chapter is correct, therefore, the United States government must bear a heavy, though by no means exclusive, burden of responsibility for the grave problems confronting the Native communities of Alaska.

CONCLUSION

There have been some indications of improvement in the quality of life of Alaska Natives during the 1970s. But there is little evidence to link these developments to the activities of the Alaska Native regional corporations. In fact, these corporations have had remarkably little impact on the day-to-day existence of the Native peoples of Alaska. At the same time, the decision to establish the regional corporations as the key element in the "machinery of settlement" outlined in PL 92–203 has produced some deeply troubling consequences. Little has been done to resolve the economic problems of the Native villages, the basic units of Native society. Rather, "it unfortunately seems that the village economies will be subject to the continued high degree of seasonality, uncertainty, and long-term instability which has characterized them for two hundred years of white contact."[101] The traditional sociocultural patterns of Native life continue to disintegrate, and there are few signs of reorganization on some new basis. Moreover, there is a rising tide of resentment and hostility in many segments of the Alaska

Native community. Whatever improvement in the quality of
life has occurred since 1971 has been outstripped by a wave of
rising expectations and a sense of confusion associated with
the disintegration of a traditional way of life. There is no
reason to doubt that the legislators who wrote the Settlement
Act were, for the most part, prepared to make a meaningful
settlement with the Alaska Natives. But as the authors of
Letters to Howard have pointed out, "The 'experts' can write
a complicated legal document like AN ACT, but it is the far
simpler and humbler folk who have to live with the
consequences."[102]

How can we account for the adoption of a settlement
producing such disruptive consequences for the Native communities of Alaska? It is tempting to approach this question
from a Marxian perspective, to look for powerful economic
forces whose interests are being served by the unfolding
consequences of the Settlement Act and to suggest the
existence of an elite that knew exactly what it was doing in
working out the "machinery of settlement" contained in the
Act. But I find it hard to accept an explanation of this sort in
the case of the Native claims settlement. Not only does this
perspective require a key role for motives that do not seem to
me to have been pervasive (at least in conscious form) in the
interactions leading to the passage of the Settlement Act. It
also imputes either an underlying purposiveness or a manipulable quality to the legislative process which does not strike
me as having been present in the case of the Native claims.

There is an alternative explanation for the adoption of a
settlement producing unforeseen and unintended consequences of a disruptive sort. Part of the explanation no doubt
lies in the complexity of all major social issues. Choices about
such issues must inevitably be made in a climate of uncertainty, and unforeseen consequences are common under such
conditions. In my judgment, however, a large part of the
explanation has to do with the character of the American
legislative process. The legislative schedule is always heavy;

there is rarely time to consider any given policy problem reflectively and in depth. The fundamental style of Congress emphasizes negotiating skills and the forging of legislative bargains rather than the formulation of coherent and internally consistent solutions for substantive problems. Many policy problems, such as the settlement of the Alaska Native claims, do not generate broad or intense interest within the legislature. Thus, while numerous members of Congress were perfectly willing to support a generally liberal settlement of these claims, they were not prepared to think about the issue in depth or to stand firm for a preferred settlement in the face of pressures to compromise arising from negotiations pertaining to other social issues. Moreover, Congress is not adept at making good use of expert knowledge relating to issues like the Native claims. Not only is there no systematic method of locating expert knowledge on such issues, but individual experts are also typically called in more for preconceived purposes of advocacy or negotiation than as sources of informed analyses and judgments. Faced with pressures to reach a legislative solution coupled with a lack of any profound understanding of the problems of the Native peoples, therefore, the legislative drafters simply resorted to familiar institutional arrangements suggested by their own training and prior experience. They laid out a system of corporations that seemed perfectly reasonable from the point of view of the dominant, white society but which would inevitably wreak havoc with the traditional way of life of the Native peoples.

It is also worth noting here that policymakers are extremely limited in their ability to influence the implementation of legislation after its passage. The obstacles to effective oversight with respect to any major piece of legislation are legion. The interests of bureaucrats in a given area may not coincide at all with the intentions of congressional policymakers, and the obstructive capacity of the bureaucracy is impressive even when it cannot pursue more positive goals effectively. In the case of the Settlement Act, sensitivity to potential charges of intervention or paternalism appear to have limited even further the ability of the legislature to affect the implementation of the Act. Thus, there is no indication that Congress was prepared to cope with the legal complications that have arisen in transferring formal title to land to the Natives, the delays that have occurred in paying out the portion of the financial settlement coming from the extraction of minerals, or the difficulties that have emerged in adapting state programs to respond to various welfare and social service needs of the Native communities.[103] Moreover, Congress has exhibited little concern about these unforeseen problems or capacity to rectify them in the years since the passage of the Settlement Act.[104]

There is nothing unique about the far-reaching impact of the unforeseen and unintended consequences flowing from PL 92-203. Similar phenomena are easy to identify in other areas.[105] The problems of unemployment associated with minimum wage laws were evidently generally unforeseen. The painful consequences of urban renewal programs for many inner city residents were apparently largely unintended. And there is no reason to suppose that Congress intended to create the current problems relating to the disposal of nuclear wastes in acting to encourage nuclear power production some years ago. Therefore, while this case study of the Alaska Native Claims Settlement Act is of substantial interest in its own right, it is also worth contemplating for what it can tell us about governmental policymaking more generally.

Three

The State as Operating Authority: The Fur Seal Act of 1966

American experience with the state as an operating authority is severely limited. The country does not have a national airline or a national railway system (with the minor exception of the Alaska Railroad), much less a national oil company. But the United States has not succeeded altogether in avoiding a role for the state as an operating authority with respect to natural resources. The Tennessee Valley Authority (TVA), a public corporation, is a major force shaping decisions about the use of the water resources of the southern part of the country. Nor is it implausible to regard the federal government as an operating authority with regard to the production of recreational values from national park lands. In some ways, however, the most intriguing example of the U.S. federal government functioning as an operating authority in the realm of natural resources involves the consumptive use of wild animals. Though it is not widely known, the United States has exercised a public monopoly over the commercial harvest of northern fur seals (*Callorhinus ursinus*) throughout most of the twentieth century.[1]

THE FUR SEAL REGIME

The commercial harvest of fur seals breeding on the Pribilof Islands has gone on with few interruptions for almost two hundred years.[2] Since 1910, this harvest has been conducted on an exclusive basis by the federal government. At the same time, the management of all northern fur seals, those associated with Robben Island and the Commander Islands, as well as the Pribilofs, has been subject to the provisions of a series of international agreements dating back to 1911. The existing agreement, the Interim Convention for the Conservation of Northern Fur Seals of 1957, is due to expire on 14 October 1980, unless extended or renegotiated.[3] While the regime established by this Convention is frequently cited as a prime example of successful resource management at the international level,[4] the impending expiration of the Convention has given rise to an extensive and often emotional debate about the proper role of the state with regard to this resource.

During the period between 1890 and 1910, the fur seal harvest became the focus of an intense controversy at the international level, commanding the attention of the leading policymakers of the great powers. By way of comparison, it seems fair to conclude not only that the issue generated more intense political concern during much of this period than the contemporary controversy over whaling but also that the recent Anglo-Icelandic cod wars have been relatively mild when contrasted with the international confrontations over the fur seals at the turn of the century. An international arbitral decision in 1893 settled certain outstanding issues pertaining to fur seals between Britain (for Canada) and the United States.[5] But this decision had no bearing on the activities of Japan and Russia, and it failed to resolve the critical issue of pelagic (or open sea) sealing. It follows that the more comprehensive Fur Seal Convention of 1911, negotiated by the United States, Britain (for Canada), Japan, and

Russia, must be understood as a hard-won international compromise intended to defuse a severe conflict that had festered for years.[6]

The key to this compromise was an agreement to treat all northern fur seal herds as common property at the international level coupled with a set of provisions allocating managerial authority over individual herds to the government of the state on whose territory the hauling grounds of a herd are located.[7] Therefore, the fur seals of the Pribilof Islands are not public property of the United States over which the federal government is entitled to exercise exclusive property rights.[8] They are owned in common with the governments of Canada, Japan, and the Soviet Union. Moreover, while the existing regime vests considerable managerial authority over the Pribilof fur seals in the U.S. federal government, it does not delegate unlimited authority to the United States. For example, the American government found it expedient and undoubtedly legally necessary to obtain agreement from the other three governments before instituting a moratorium on commercial harvesting of fur seals on Saint George Island in 1973. Under the existing regime, there can be little doubt that the consent of the other owners would be required before the United States, acting in its capacity as manager, could make major changes in current management practices (for example, terminating the commercial harvest) pertaining to the Pribilof fur seals.[9]

Equally important is the establishment by the existing regime, both in its 1911 and in its 1957 versions, of a system of *restricted* common property.[10] That is, the basic condition of common property is accompanied by definite rules together with well-defined procedures for modifying these rules. The most important rule of this regime is a total ban on pelagic sealing, with the exception of highly restricted subsistence harvesting on the part of Native peoples. Pelagic sealing was not only the critical cause of the severe depletion of fur seal stocks prior to 1911, it is also a highly inefficient practice from an economic point of view.[11] A second important rule stipulates that all commercial harvesting on land is to be carried out by the United States on the Pribilofs and by the Soviet Union on Robben Island and the Commanders.[12] In return for these concessions, Canada and Japan obtained a rule allocating all sealskins taken by the United States and the Soviet Union. This is the 70–15–15 formula set forth in Article IX of the 1957 Convention. Both the United States and the Soviet Union agree to delivery 15 percent of all sealskins taken under their jurisdiction to Canada and Japan respectively. Finally, there is an important rule under which all the co-owners commit themselves to carry out extensive research relating to the management of fur seals and to coordinate their scientific research programs in this area (Art. II). The implementation of this rule has been the principal concern of the International North Pacific Fur Seal Commission established under Article V of the 1957 Convention.[13]

The Interim Convention was a product of the maximum sustained yield (MSY) era in renewable resource management. Thus, the preamble of the Convention states that fur seal populations are to be "brought to and maintained at the levels which will provide the greatest harvest year after year." It is now widely understood that MSY is apt to be impossible to calculate with any precision under real-world conditions, whether or not it is considered desirable as a normative goal.[14] The factors leading to this conclusion (for example, interdependencies among separate species, changing ecosystems, practical problems in monitoring populations) are just as troublesome for fur seals as they are with respect to other renewable resources. Nevertheless, MSY remains the official management objective of the existing fur seal regime.[15]

There are several ways of looking at the record of this international regime. Overall, the northern fur seal has made a remarkable comeback under its aegis. The Pribilof herds, for example, which were down to 200 to 300 thousand in 1911, now number approximately 1.4 million.[16] In fact, the size of the herds was deliberately reduced from an even higher level during the late 1950s and early 1960s. But subsequent changes in the ecosystem of the central Bering Sea make it unlikely that the Pribilof herds could be rebuilt to their pre-1956 level of about 2.25 million, and it is probable that the current size of these herds is not drastically below the carrying capacity of this ecosystem.[17] The commercial harvest of Pribilof fur seals has been limited to nonbreeding males since the end of the herd reduction program in the middle 1960s. This harvest now runs in the range of 25,000 to 30,000 animals a year, down from an average of closer to 60,000 prior to the herd reduction program and the termination of commercial harvesting on Saint George.[18]

As the preceding paragraph implies, the management objective of MSY has been substantially modified in practice. The herd reduction program initiated in 1956 has been variously justified as a means of increasing the productivity of the Pribilof herds or as a measure required to prevent the fur seals from exceeding the (declining) carrying capacity of the ecosystem. But there is good reason to interpret it largely as a response to Japanese fears about possible interference by fur seals with the growing Japanese high seas fisheries of the Bering Sea.[19] The public rationale for the moratorium on commercial harvesting on Saint George starting in 1973 emphasized the desirability of conducting systematic research contrasting the population dynamics of exploited and unexploited fur seal herds. But it is widely believed that one important factor leading to the Saint George moratorium was a desire on the part of the U.S. federal government to accommodate pressures from several preservationist groups. However this may be, it seems evident that the requirements of attaining MSY do not dictate management decisions under the fur seal regime and that this is an area in which political considerations have been prominent for many years.

It is also worth noting that some fur seals are killed each year as a by-catch in high seas fishing operations; others become victims of discarded nets or other debris associated with high seas fishing. This fact has not been widely publicized, and there is no way to determine exactly how many fur seals are killed in this way. It is probable, however, that mortalities from all these sources currently run in the range of 5,000 to 10,000 a year. In fact, it is probable that seal mortalities attributable to high seas fishing have declined somewhat as a result of recent changes in the International North Pacific Fisheries Convention under which the Japanese no longer take salmon in the area between 175° W and 175° E.[20] This is so because fur seals consume salmon in quantity and the gear used in high seas salmon fishing is dangerous to fur seals. Nevertheless, inadvertent seal mortalities attributable to these sources are certainly not trivial, and this problem requires careful consideration in the future.

The international fur seal regime is supplemented by national systems of administration promulgated by the United States for the Pribilof Islands and the Soviet Union for Robben Island and the Commander Islands. During the period between 1870 and 1910, the United States leased the right to harvest fur seals on the Pribilofs to one or another private corporation on the basis of twenty-year leases. Under the terms of the Fur Seal Act of 1910 (PL 61–146, 36 Stat. 326), however, the U.S. federal government set itself up as an operating authority with the exclusive right to harvest fur seals commercially and to sell their skins. The current administrative system for the Pribilofs is set forth in the Fur Seal Act of 1966 (PL 89–702, 80 Stat. 1091, 16 USC 1151 et. seq.), which implements the Interim Convention of 1957 as far as the United States is concerned. The administrative system divides naturally into an arrangement for the actual harvest of seals and a set of provisions for the support of the Aleut communities of Saint Paul and Saint George. Both arrangements are under the operational control of the Pribilof Islands Program, an arm of the National Marine Fisheries Service (NMFS) located in the U.S. Department of Commerce.

The harvesting system set up under PL 89-702 is straightforward. The federal government continues to serve as an operating authority for this activity; it does not contract out the seal harvest. Virtually all labor required to carry out the harvest (except the labor of supervisory personnel) is obtained by hiring Natives from Saint Paul and Saint George under the rules pertaining to Wage Board employees.[21] The sealskins are shipped to South Carolina for tanning, finishing, and sale at auction by the Fouke Fur Company. The federal government retains ownership of the skins until final sale, compensating the Fouke Company on a fee basis.[22] In contrast, the government has contracted out the disposition of the by-products of the harvest—mainly seal carcasses—for some years. Initially, the by-products contract was held by a private firm called Oregon-Alaska Marine Products, which installed equipment in a government-built processing plant on Saint Paul to handle its operation. In 1978, however, this operation was taken over by the Tanadgusix Corporation, the village corporation for Saint Paul created under the terms of the Alaska Native Claims Settlement Act of 1971 (PL 92-203, 85 Stat. 688, 43 USC 1601 et seq.). While it is probably accurate to say that a contractual relationship concerning the by-products operation exists between Tanadgusix and NMFS, the terms of this contract are not entirely clear. This is a matter that unquestionably requires clarification at the present time.

Historically, the communities of Saint Paul and Saint George exhibited all the characteristics of company towns.[23] If anything, this condition appears to have become more pronounced after the federal government took over the commercial harvest of fur seals in 1910. While this ensured effective government control over the seal harvest, it also led to almost total dependence of Saint Paul and Saint George on the federal government and a gradual expansion of federal obligations toward these communities and their permanent residents.[24] One of the objectives of the Fur Seal Act of 1966 was to reverse this pattern of growing dependence and to encourage self-sufficiency and local self-government on the Pribilofs (sec. 206). Some progress has been made toward the achievement of these objectives. Saint Paul is now incorporated as a second class city under the laws of the state of Alaska.[25] Land and individual homes are being conveyed to the Native peoples under the terms of the Native Claims Settlement Act. The city of Saint Paul has begun to take over certain municipal functions (for example, garbage disposal, road maintenance, law enforcement). And the activities of Tanadgusix and Tanaq (the village corporation for Saint George) are beginning to offer some new economic options to the two communities. Nevertheless, Saint Paul and especially Saint George remain heavily dependent on the federal government not only economically but also in the realms of health, welfare, and general community support. Under the terms of PL 89–702, the government clearly has extensive obligations toward these communities, obligations that are not legally tied to the continuation of the commercial harvest of fur seals. That is, federal obligations toward Saint Paul and Saint George would not be reduced at all if the seal harvest were to cease. Of course, Congress could amend PL 89–702 to reduce or eliminate these obligations. But the modern history of the Pribilofs offers a compelling moral basis for these obligations, and any move to rescind them against the wishes of the people of the Pribilofs would be hard to justify.[26]

All proceeds accruing to the federal government from the sale of sealskins go into the Pribilof Islands Fund set up in the U.S. Treasury by section 407 of PL 89–702. This money is used not only to cover the actual cost of harvesting the fur seals but also to pay for other expenses of the Pribilof Islands Program. That is, the money generated by the sealskin industry goes to pay for the obligations referred to in the preceding paragraph as well as to pay the costs of the industry itself.[27] Should any surplus remain after covering all expenses, 30 percent of the residual funds are retained by the federal government while 70 percent of these funds go to the state of

Alaska under the terms of section 6(e) of the Alaska Statehood Act of 1958 (PL 85–508, 72 Stat. 334). Alaska received payments from the Pribilof Islands Fund through 1969. Since then, profits from the seal harvest have been insufficient to cover all expenses of the Pribilof Islands Program in the realms of welfare, education, and general community support. Consequently, the state has received no payments under PL 85–508, and the Pribilof Islands Program has had to seek separate appropriations from Congress to cover the obligations assumed in PL 89–702.

CONSUMPTIVE USE

Consumptive use of wild animals encompasses all intentional killing for subsistence, sport, or commercial purposes. Consumptive use, therefore, is to be contrasted with amenity or nonconsumptive use involving such things as observation by naturalists, photography, and general aesthetic enjoyment.[28] In the case of the northern fur seal, the key issue in this realm concerns the commercial harvest of sealskins. There is no sport hunting of fur seals, and the traditional subsistence harvest is minimal.[29] Accordingly, we must confront the following question: should the commercial harvest of Pribilof fur seals be allowed to continue or should we endeavor to terminate it either immediately or gradually on some phased basis?

I do not believe it is possible to resolve this question by reference to some general principle or rule. That is, it does not strike me as helpful to assert dogmatically that consumptive use of wild animals is never acceptable or always acceptable and then to resolve the fur seal question through a simple application of this rule. Rather, it is necessary to examine the pros and cons of consumptive use on a case-by-case basis. What are the principle arguments for and against terminating the commercial harvest of Pribilof fur seals and how do these arguments stack up against each other? Proceeding in this fashion, I have come to the conclusion that the arguments in favor of continuing the commercial harvest of

Pribilof fur seals outweigh those supporting the termination of this harvest. Here, I endeavor to present these arguments and to justify my conclusion. Consider first the case for terminating the commercial harvest of Pribilof fur seals. It is worth differentiating several specific arguments in this case, though they are often deployed simultaneously by advocates of termination.

Preservationism

Some proponents of termination oppose all killing of animals—wild or otherwise—on the part of humans. This argument divides in turn into several major strands. In some cases, it rests on simple affection or admiration for animals. But this posture immediately invites difficult questions about demarcation. If consumptive use of fur seals is unacceptable, what about deer or sheep or cattle? Alternatively, the preservationist perspective is sometimes rooted in aesthetic considerations. Thus, there are those who would like to see the creation of a Pribilof Islands seal sanctuary under which the commercial harvest would be abandoned in favor of an unexploited population available for observation by naturalists.[30] Notice, however, that this is ultimately a class-based point of view. Those likely to visit a seal sanctuary would inevitably be drawn largely from the upper and upper middle classes while those whose interests would be hurt by the termination of the seal harvest would be occupants of lower social strata. Yet another basis for the preservationist perspective involves right-to-life principles. There are those who argue that individual animals possess a right to life and that this entails an obligation on the part of humans to refrain from killing them, except perhaps in extreme situations involving self-defense.[31] This line of thinking arises from an explicit concern for individual animals in contrast to the focus on maintaining healthy animal populations which underlies most professional game management programs. Further, efforts to extend the domain of rights beyond the category of human beings are highly controversial. They will encounter heavy opposition, for example, from those who emphasize factors like conscious discretion in exercising rights as a qualification for holding rights.[32]

Further Distinctions

It is not necessary to subscribe to some version of preservationism to favor terminating the commercial harvest of Pribilof fur seals. Several additional distinctions will serve to clarify this proposition. To begin with, it is possible to draw a distinction between wild animals and domestic animals and to oppose consumptive use of wild animals. But this argument is hard to accept. After all, domestic animals are more likely to become objects of human affection than wild animals, and they are more often treated as distinct individuals as well. Next, some may wish to distinguish between types of animals, opposing consumptive use of certain animals but sanctioning consumptive use of others. This might serve as a basis for the now fashionable opposition to consumptive use of whales and elephants. But where are we to draw the line in the spectrum of animals, and on which side of the line would fur seals fall? Also, is this merely a way of saying that certain animals (for example, large and dramatic ones) tend to capture the human imagination more easily than others? Yet another distinction involves the difference between sport hunting and commercial harvesting of wild animals. But it is hard to see any persuasive reason to prefer sport hunting over commercial harvesting. Sport hunting encompasses an ineradicable element of killing for pleasure whereas commercial harvesting has an economic motivation and may provide a much needed industrial base for local communities. Finally, there is a distinction relating to the purposes for which animals are killed. Some of the opposition to the Pribilof fur seal harvest, for example, stems from the proposition that consumptive use of wild animals is unacceptable when they are used to produce luxury items—in this case sealskin coats.[33] The idea here is that necessities and luxuries are fundamentally different and that consumptive use must be confined to cases of necessity. But what is necessity? It turns out that there is a large element of subjectivity or cultural relativism associated with answers to this question.[34] Given the possibilities of substitution, it is even difficult to argue that consumptive use of any specific animal is necessary as a source of protein.

Inhumane Treatment

Another argument against the commercial harvest of Pribilof fur seals rests on the proposition that the harvest involves inhumane treatment of animals. Of course, some may argue that any killing of animals is inhumane by definition, in which case this becomes a right-to-life issue and does not require separate treatment here. If killing is not automatically ruled out under the heading of inhumane treatment, however, the issue becomes a matter of the technique employed in conducting the harvest. The seal harvest involves stunning and exsanguination (bleeding) by cutting the main vessels to the heart. This technique has been much debated, and extensive experiments with other techniques of killing have been carried out. No one would argue that killing animals is an attractive process under any circumstances. But it is generally agreed that stunning causes less pain and suffering to the seals than other available methods of killing.[35]

Economics of Sealing

The Pribilof fur seal harvest is sometimes opposed on the grounds that it is unprofitable and consequently constitutes an unnecessary drain on the federal treasury.[36] Unfortunately, this argument rests on a serious misconception. During fiscal year 1976 and fiscal year 1977 (the latest years for which complete figures are available), the costs of harvesting and processing sealskins ran to $353,800 and $273,000, while federal receipts from the sale of sealskins amounted to

$1,624,427 and $1,617,225 respectively. Treated strictly as a business, therefore, the commercial harvest of fur seals yielded profits of $1,270,627 for fiscal year 1976 and $1,343,325 for fiscal year 1977. Moreover, these profits were obtained although the magnitude of the harvest has been deliberately reduced since 1956 for noneconomic reasons, and harvesting and processing are currently conducted on an intentionally inefficient basis to protect jobs on Saint Paul. What is true is that the Pribilof Islands Program as a whole has run a deficit (i.e. required appropriations in excess of receipts from the sale of sealskins) since 1970. This deficit amounted to $2,303,773 in fiscal year 1976 and $3,695,275 in fiscal year 1977. This means that total payments to meet federal obligations to the communities of Saint Paul and Saint George exceeded receipts from the sale of sealskins by these amounts. But the critical point here is that these deficits would increase, at least in the short run, if the seal harvest were terminated. As I pointed out previously, federal obligations relating to health, welfare, and general community support on the Pribilofs are mandated by PL 89–702, and they are not tied to the continuation of the seal harvest. At the same time, the cessation of the harvest would eliminate receipts from the sale of sealskins and force the federal government to devise makeshift employment opportunities on Saint Paul. The experience of Saint George since the 1973 moratorium offers ample support for this analysis.

Economic Alternatives

Those who favor terminating the Pribilof seal harvest also argue that there are straightforward economic alternatives to sealing that could be developed to sustain the local economy following the cessation of sealing.[37] All sides agree that the most promising alternative is the development of a Bering Sea bottom fishery and crab fishery based largely on Saint Paul. This would give rise to a need for processing facilities and vessel supply operations as well as for harvesting capabilities as such. In fact, the fisheries lying to the north and west of the Pribilofs are rich, and the Fishery Conservation and Management Act of 1976 (PL 94-265, 90 Stat. 331, 16 USC 1801 et seq.) encourages developments along these lines.[38] But there are substantial problems with this option. Under the best of circumstances, the evolution of a flourishing fishery based on the Pribilofs would take ten to fifteen years. The proposed boat harbor on Saint Paul would have to be installed.[39] Adequate equipment and shore-based facilities would have to be acquired. Skill and experience pertaining to high seas fishing, now almost totally lacking among the residents of the Pribilofs, would take time to develop. There is a good chance that processing facilities would fall under the control of outsiders with little interest in the welfare of the communities of Saint Paul and Saint George. And the marine fisheries have a well-earned reputation for volatility, which makes them somewhat unreliable as an economic base for rural communities. In this context, it is also pertinent that the initial wave of enthusiasm for bottom fishing off Alaska following the passage of PL 94-265 is now being tempered by realistic assessments of the difficulties associated with this industry. Beyond this, it is likely that a growing fishing industry based on the Pribilofs would transform Saint George and especially Saint Paul within fifteen years. Not only would this lead to drastic changes in the socioeconomic character of the two communities, it would also precipitate serious changes in both the marine and terrestrial portions of the ecosystem inhabited by the fur seals. This means that it is probable that the overall carrying capacity of the ecosystem would decline further. A potential result is that what began as an effort to save seals would lead over time to a reduction in the total population of fur seals.

The other prominent economic alternative for the Pribilofs involves oil and gas development on the outer continental shelf (OCS). In fact, the so-called Saint George basin lying south of the Pribilofs is regarded as promising by many industry sources, and a lease sale in this area is tentatively scheduled for the early 1980s. If anything, this alternative seems even more ominous from the point of view of the fur seals as well as from the perspective of the local residents of Saint George and Saint Paul. The experiences of other onshore communities are hardly encouraging, and the prospect of a lease sale in the Saint George basin has (not surprisingly) aroused considerable anxiety on the Pribilofs. Of course, the disruptive prospects of bottom fishing and OCS development are not mutually exclusive; the Pribilofs could well experience both during the 1980s.

There are, then, several separate arguments included in the case for terminating the commercial harvest of Pribilof fur seals. While some of these arguments rest on value judgments and certainly should not be dismissed lightly, many of them strike me as flawed to a more or less serious extent. But this is only one side of the debate over the seal harvest. Turn now to the case for continuing the commercial harvest of fur seals on the Pribilofs.

Population Dynamics

The fur seal herds of the Pribilofs are large, stable, and not drastically below the current carrying capacity of the ecosystem.[40] These herds have remained stable at approximately 1.4 to 1.5 million animals since the end of the herd reduction program in the 1960s. The annual production of pups now runs in the proper range to maintain this population size. In general, the herds are thought to be distinctly healthy. That is, the level of natural mortality is not unusually high and the pregnancy rate among breeding females is high.[41] Under the circumstances, no serious observer would argue that there is any danger to the Pribilof herds associated with a policy of continuing the commercial harvest on a controlled basis. In this context, experience with the fur seals of Saint George since the 1973 moratorium is instructive. The Saint George herd has not increased in size since 1973. While it is premature to speak of significant trends, there has been a slight decline in productivity in this herd in recent years. It is not possible at this time to advance a substantiated explanation of this phenomenon. But the Saint George situation certainly lends support to the argument that human predation is not now a major determinant of overall population size for the northern fur seal.

Environmental Impacts

There are two scenarios concerning the probable environmental impacts of terminating the seal harvest. One might be labeled the Saint George scenario after the experience since the 1973 moratorium. It suggests that the Pribilof seal herds would not increase in size following the cessation of sealing and might even decline somewhat over time. The other scenario projects a substantial increase in the Saint Paul herd, at least in the short run. But what would be the effect of such a development over a longer time period? Some argue that the seal populatoin would be likely to build up to a natural maximum and then crash, as has happened repeatedly with reindeer herds in Alaska and may now be happening with Bering Sea walrus populations. But most observers do not attach a high probability to this prospect. Rather, they predict increasing volatility in the seal herds coupled with a gradual return of the population to a point near the current level. This increased volatility might take the form of rising levels of natural mortality in the entire population or of large fluctuations from one year class to another. Moreover, an increased seal population could well interfere with efforts to develop extensive fisheries based on the Pribilof Islands or along the Aleutian chain.[42] In this case, a political battle would ensue, and it is certainly not safe to assume that the seals would emerge as the winners. Whichever of these scenarios should prove more accurate, it is hard to construct a persuasive argument against the seal harvest on environmental grounds. Naturally, this will hardly impress those who oppose the harvest on the basis of some variety of preservationism. But for those who approach wildlife management in terms of the

goal of maintaining healthy and stable populations of animals, a policy of continuing the seal harvest has much to
recommend it.

Predator / Prey Relationships

Predatory behavior is natural and widespread throughout the animal world. The fur seal itself is a highly effective
predator consuming large quantities of fish and other marine
organisms on a continuous basis,[43] and man is arguably the
predator par excellence of the animal kingdom. Accordingly,
there is nothing unnatural or abnormal about the consumptive use of wild animals. It is true that commercial sealing
does not qualify as a subsistence operation in any narrow
sense of that term. But the meaning of subsistence is notori-
ously difficult to capture under contemporary conditions, and
the seal harvest has made a critical contribution to the economic and social well-being of the Pribilof communities over
a long period. Without doubt, the situation would be different if human predation had become a threat to the continued
viability of the fur seal herds. But as I have already indicated,
not only is this not the case, it is also probable that alternative
economic activities would pose greater threats to the fur seals
over time even though they did not involve any direct or
intentional killing of seals. From this perspective, opposition
to commercial sealing takes on a quality of pointless senti-
mentalism. It has little justification in terms of any conception of stewardship,[44] and attempts to invest it with an air of
moral superiority rest on a misconception of the nature of
man.

Cultural Significance

Much has been made recently of the question of whether
or not the Native peoples of Saint Paul and Saint George
have a profound "spiritual" relationship to the harvest of fur
seals.[45] But it is hard to make sense of this question in the
context of communities whose development has been shaped

by one or another dominant white society for several centuries and whose character is now changing rapidly in many ways. Nonetheless, several observations of a cultural nature are pertinent. The Aleut peoples of Saint Paul are unanimously and profoundly committed to the continuation of the seal harvest. There is no doubt that they would resent deeply an outside decision to terminate the harvest, especially if it were arrived at by distant authorities making little effort to consult them seriously about the issue. This would simply constitute one more demonstration of the long-established callousness and insensitivity of dominant white societies toward the feelings and desires of Native peoples. Such a development would certainly be disturbing in light of the unfortunate record of the U.S. federal government in its dealings with the peoples of the Pribilofs. Even more important, such an insensitive action would hardly be conducive to the development of self-assurance and self-sufficiency among the Native peoples of the Pribilofs, the avowed policy of the federal government at least since the passage of the Fur Seal Act of 1966. With all due respect to the normative precepts underlying the views of those who oppose the continuation of the seal harvest, therefore, I believe it is of great importance to bear in mind the normative considerations calling for the adoption of a sensitive posture toward the desires of a group of people who have manifestly experienced ill treatment in the past.

Economic Issues

Terminating the fur seal harvest would produce severe economic dislocation on the Pribilofs in the short run and probably the long run as well. At present, sealing is the only significant industry on Saint Paul; there is no significant industry on Saint George. While this industry does not dominate the economy of the island as much as it once did, it still accounts for approximately two-thirds of the local employment opportunities.[46] As I have already suggested, there are economic alternatives for the Pribilofs. Realistically, however, we must assume that it would take ten to fifteen years to develop a flourishing fishing industry based on a new boat harbor at Saint Paul or, for that matter, on the existing harbor at Chernofski on Unalaska Island.[47] Consequently, a cessation of the seal harvest would produce considerable economic dislocation in the short run, and it would sharply increase Saint Paul's dependence on the federal government. Not only would this run directly counter to the goals articulated in PL 89-702, it would also have unfortunate sociocultural consequences as the experience of Saint George in the period since 1973 suggests. Moreover, the long-run economic implications of terminating the fur seal harvest might prove quite unattractive even if alternative industries were to emerge quickly. Sealing has several desirable features in comparison to other industries. It is a stable, self-contained industry based on a renewable resource. Managed properly, it can be carried on indefinitely with little damage to the ecosystem. And it is labor intensive rather than energy intensive.[48] Contrast this with either of the principal alternatives: a modern, mechanized fishery or OCS development. Not only would these alternatives be likely to transform the communities of Saint George and Saint Paul in socioeconomic terms, they would also generate far greater threats to the ecosystem than a modest seal harvest. The likelihood of serious disruption along these lines would only increase to the extent that pressures mount to pursue such economic alternatives hastily with heavy reliance on external capital and expertise and little effective control on the part of the local communities.[49] The Pribilofs will experience rapid change during the 1980s regardless of what is decided about the future of the fur seal harvest. But a decision to terminate the harvest would constitute a powerful spur to developments whose unintended disruptive consequences could well become a source of widespread dismay within ten to fifteen years.

International Cooperation

The existing regime for the fur seals is a prominent example of successful resource management at the international level. Under its aegis, the fur seal herds have returned from severe depletion to a condition of health and stability not drastically below the carrying capacity of the relevant ecosystem. Moreover, the regime has the distinction of being the oldest operative arrangement for resource management at the international level. Not surprisingly, the other parties to the arrangement, Canada, Japan, and the Soviet Union, have expressed satisfaction with the regime and would like to see it extended without fundamental changes. Under the circumstances, an American move to terminate the Pribilof seal harvest and to withdraw unilaterally from the international fur seal regime would inevitably be construed as an abrupt and seemingly careless abandonment of a successful international resource regime. Such a move could hardly have beneficial consequences from the point of view of future efforts to encourage international cooperation with respect to the management of natural resources. To make matters worse, the recent posture of the United States regarding marine resources has been distinctly discouraging from the perspective of those desiring to promote genuine international cooperation in the use of natural resources.[50] A willingness now to sacrifice a successful and long-standing international regime to the demands of relatively small groups of preservationists would only add to the emerging record of American unilateralism in this realm.

Legal Implications

It is doubtful whether the United States has the right to terminate the Pribilof seal harvest over the objections of the other parties to the Interim Convention of 1957. As I pointed out earlier, the United States does not possess exclusive property rights to the Pribilof fur seals; even its management authority with respect to these animals is by no means unlimited. And it would be difficult to construct a persuasive legal case for the proposition that one co-owner of common property is entitled to make fundamental decisions about the disposition of the property regardless of the desires of the other co-owners. Of course, the United States is in a position to ignore these legal problems and to impose its will concerning this issue because the Pribilof Islands belong to the United States and the United States is a leading great power. But this would constitute a unilateral expropriation of well-established rights held by other states and this type of behavior is one that the United States typically castigates on the part of others. In purely pragmatic terms, the United States has strong incentives to think twice about unilateral moves of this sort in an increasingly interdependent world in which other states have a growing capacity to damage American interests.[51] It has been suggested that these legal problems could be avoided by adopting a policy of discontinuing the 70 percent of the seal harvest to which the United States is entitled under the Convention formula while continuing to take and to transmit the 30 percent to which Canada and Japan are entitled. But it is hard to interpret this as anything other than a ploy on the part of those who wish to terminate the commercial harvest altogether. An action of this sort would violate the management philosophy of the Convention, and it would exceed the management authority of the United States under the Convention if carried out unilaterally. The consequent reduction in the flow of sealskins would severely damage the Fouke Company,[52] and it would dislocate the economy of Saint Paul so severely that it would be necessary to proceed forthwith with the economic alternatives previously discussed. In short, it would create an inherently unstable situation that would lead to a total cessation of the commercial harvest in relatively short order. Since this outcome is predictable *ex ante,* it is hard to see how such a move would alleviate the legal problems mentioned above.

Management Alternatives

How would the fur seal herds be managed in the wake of
an American withdrawal from the existing regime coupled
with a termination of the commercial harvest? It is widely
assumed that all fur seals within the American fishery conservation zone (FCZ) would then come under the terms of the
Marine Mammals Protection Act of 1972 (PL 92–522, 86 Stat.
1027, 16 USC 1631 et seq.).[53] While such a development is
regarded as desirable by many who oppose the commercial
harvest of fur seals, it is not without serious drawbacks. Not
only does the Marine Mammals Protection Act (MMPA)
establish a dangerously inflexible management system for
marine mammals, it also contains far more open-ended
provisions for direct harvest by Native peoples than Article
VII of the 1957 Convention and section 102 of PL 89–702.[54]
In fact, the Aleuts of Saint George and Saint Paul would
almost certainly be able to expand their unsupervised harvest
of fur seals dramatically under the arrangement. At the same
time, it is doubtful whether the basic assumption underlying
this scenario is valid. The compromise of 1911 ended a period
of severe international conflict over the fur seals by explicitly
establishing a system of common property rights in these
animals. Under the circumstances, there is no reason to
assume that the other co-owners would simply acquiesce
passively in a move on the part of the United States which
would amount to a unilateral expropriation of some of their
rights in the fur seals.[55] Again, the United States might get
away with such a move as a matter of power politics. But the
costs of doing so—indirect as well as direct—would probably
be substantial. In the event that the other co-owners refused
to acquiesce in the application of the MMPA to fur seals
within the American fishery conservation zone, a dangerous
situation would arise in which efforts to resume pelagic sealing might occur. Moreover, under either of these scenarios
there would be additional problems. The fur seals would not

be protected outside the American FCZ. It turns out that this is a more serious problem than it may at first appear since in any given year up to 20 percent of the Pribilof fur seals are thought to migrate westward through Asian waters and beyond the American FCZ rather than through North American waters.[56] The United States would also lose any prospect of influencing the management of fur seals on Robben Island and the Commanders following withdrawal from the existing regime. Since these herds have apparently been somewhat less carefully managed than the Pribilof herds over the last several decades, this may appear to some as a disturbing development.[57] All in all, then, the management situation for fur seals that would arise as a consequence of American withdrawal from the existing regime in order to terminate the Pribilof seal harvest would be ambiguous at best and might well generate deeply disturbing results.

Where does all this leave us with respect to the basic question concerning consumptive use of fur seals posed at the beginning of this section? There is no simple metric in terms of which to compute values for the various arguments reviewed above. Therefore, it is not possible to arrive at a policy decision about the future of the Pribilof fur seal harvest through an application of benefit/cost analysis.[58] In addition, there is no reason to assume that all the arguments I have reviewed should be weighted equally in any effort to arrive at a policy decision. Of course, the weights to be attached to many of the arguments must ultimately rest on value judgments; it is possible to arrive at virtually any conclusion about the Pribilof seal harvest through a suitable adjustment of these weights. It follows not only that we must not dismiss the policy recommendations of any interested group cavalierly, but also that we must constantly guard against pressures from those inclined to manipulate the weights attached to various arguments in an effort to rationalize some predetermined policy prescription.

In my judgment, however, the arguments in favor of

continuing the Pribilof fur seal harvest outweigh those supporting termination, at least at this time. As I have already
suggested, many of the arguments favoring termination are
more or less severely flawed in their application to the fur seal
situation. At the same time, the arguments favoring continuation are substantial. The Pribilof herds are stable and
healthy. Both the economic and the sociocultural dislocations
associated with termination would be severe. The economic
alternatives that would emerge in due course might well pose
serious threats to the relevant ecosystem, whereas the seal
harvest is generally compatible with the existing ecosystem.
And the international consequences of a unilateral American
move to terminate the seal harvest would be disruptive and
disturbing. It follows that the Pribilof seal harvest should
continue and that the international fur seal regime should be
extended. Several possible modifications of specific features
of this regime are outlined below.

THE SPECIAL CASE OF SAINT GEORGE

Before going on to other matters, I want to set forth a
few additional observations pertaining to the special case of
Saint George. As I indicated earlier, there has been no
commercial harvest of fur seals on Saint George since 1972.
The Saint George moratorium was proposed by the United
States and approved by the International North Pacific Fur
Seal Commission at its 1973 meeting. While the public justification for this moratorium emphasized research needs, it is
widely believed that behind-the-scenes pressures exercised by
certain preservationist groups played an important role in this
decision. No serious attempt was made in connection with
the decision to consult the people of Saint George or to
consider their point of view. In fact, no concerted effort has
been made to this day to explain the moratorium in terms
that are comprehensible to the residents of Saint George.[59]
Additionally, the moratorium was only one of a series of

rather heavy-handed actions imposed on Saint George by the federal government. During the 1960s, the government made a substantial effort to pressure the residents of Saint George into abandoning their community and relocating on Saint Paul, only gradually relenting and acquiescing in the continued existence of the community of Saint George.[60] Though the obligations toward Saint George assumed in PL 89–702 have not been abandoned since 1973, no significant effort has been made to assist the people of Saint George in developing meaningful economic alternatives to overcome the dislocation caused by the termination of the seal harvest.

What have the consequences of the Saint George moratorium been? Some worthwhile research has been carried on concerning the population dynamics of exploited versus unexploited fur seal herds. The Saint George seal herd is generally healthy, though it has not grown since 1973. The impact of the moratorium on the community of Saint George, by contrast, has been severe and disturbing. The sense of dependence of community members on the federal government has increased markedly. Most jobs are not only fully controlled by the federal government; many of them are also little more than forms of disguised unemployment. Not surprisingly, resentment toward a remote government that exhibits little sensitivity to local conditions is widespread and often intense. Enforced dependence has hardly proved a good recipe for the development of growing self-esteem and self-assurance among the people of Saint George.

Is the continuation of the Saint George moratorium justifiable at this juncture? Should a decision be reached to terminate all commercial harvesting of Pribilof fur seals, it would of course hardly make sense to treat the Saint George situation as a special case. Barring this, however, I find it difficult to construct a compelling case for the continuation of the moratorium. The issue comes down to a trade-off between the benefits of research and the welfare of the community of Saint George. It is not self-evident that the claims of research should receive precedence under any circumstances. But the current situation with respect to Saint George seems especially unfavorable to the claims of research. The research permitted by the moratorium, while certainly useful, is not critical to the maintenance of the Pribilof seal herds at this time. In any case, the research program is not currently being pursued with notable vigor.[61] By contrast, the negative impact of the moratorium on the community is severe and continuous. Therefore, I would favor lifting the Saint George moratorium in conjunction with a renewed commitment to the principal features of the international fur seal regime.

CONDUCTING THE HARVEST

Assume now that the commercial harvest of Pribilof fur seals continues. What is the preferred method of conducting this harvest? Under the Fur Seal Act of 1910, the U.S. federal government set itself up as an operating authority with a monopoly over the harvest of Pribilof fur seals. While this arrangement is not required under the terms of the international regime, it has remained in force during the intervening years, currently receiving legal expression in sections 101 and 104 of PL 89–702. So far as I know, this arrangement is unique in the United States. Many natural resources are publicly owned or subject to the management authority of the federal government. And there are other cases in which the federal government has set itself up as an operating authority, usually through the medium of a public corporation (for example, the TVA). But there is no other example of the government exercising a monopoly over the actual exploitation of a renewable resource. This unique arrangement would be well worth examining under any circumstances. In the case of the Pribilof fur seals, the arrangement has some serious drawbacks, and there are good reasons to question whether it constitutes the preferred method of organizing the harvest in the future—whether or not it did in the past. Here

I canvass the principal options for the conduct of the fur seal harvest, to contrast these options with the current system and to reach some conclusion about a preferred method for the future.

Individual Harvesters

A simple arrangement would be to allow individuals to harvest fur seals for commercial purposes on their own initiative. Of course, such a system would require definite rules. Pelagic sealing would be prohibited; an overall annual quota or some other device to limit the harvest would be needed, and it might be desirable to require individuals intending to harvest seals commercially to obtain permits.[62] In addition, a strong case could be made for restricting the issuance of permits to individual Natives resident on Saint Paul or Saint George. The result would be a harvesting system resembling the arrangement for marine fishing set forth in PL 94-265. It would appeal to those who believe in individual initiative, and it would not encourage disruptive economic development on the Pribilofs. Nevertheless, this method of conducting the harvest has severe drawbacks, at least as applied to the Pribilof seal harvest. There is no history of individual initiative in sealing in these communities. In many ways, such a system would conflict with the traditional Aleut culture or life-style, which emphasizes cooperation and community action rather than individualism and the growth of independent entrepreneurship. Under the arrangement, it would be extremely difficult to enforce regulations designed to ensure the continued viability of the resource. Enforcement efforts would have to extend to numerous individuals rather than focusing on a single agency or enterprise. And in any case, processing would still require a centralized operation since individuals would lack the ability to process and ship sealskins efficiently. Under the circumstances, I conclude that this method of organizing the harvest should not be adopted, though it is not entirely lacking in attractive features.

Private Industry

An alternative arrangement would be for the federal
government to negotiate leases with one or more private
corporations to harvest Pribilof fur seals under specified
conditions. Numerous variations on this basic theme are
possible depending upon the specific conditions incorporated
in the leases. As with outer continental shelf (OCS) leasing, it
would be feasible to choose among private corporations either
on the basis of administrative decisions coupled with work
obligation permits or on the basis of some form of competitive bidding.[63] In fact, this type of arrangement has already
been tried in conjunction with the commercial harvest of fur
seals. Between 1870 and 1910, the federal government
entered into two twenty-year leases, first with the Alaska
Commercial Company and then with the North American
Commercial Company, for the harvest of Pribilof fur seals
and the support of the Aleut communities of Saint Paul and
Saint George. But the problems with this option are so severe
that it can hardly be regarded as a serious possibility at this
time. The record compiled under this arrangement between
1870 and 1910 was generally dismal. The private corporations
presided over a period of rapid decline in the fur seal herds,
though it is true that pelagic sealing was a key factor in this
decline and that the leaseholders were not in a position to
control pelagic sealing. Experience in other areas suggests that
it is not easy to achieve effective enforcement of environmental regulations when the subjects of these regulations are
influential private corporations.[64] Reliance on outside corporations to harvest fur seals would introduce a major new force
into the political economy of the Pribilofs. And it is inevitable that these corporations would be concerned primarily
with profit maximization rather than promoting the development of self-confidence and economic self-sufficiency in the
Aleut communities. Under the circumstances, it is safe to
assume that this option would be unpopular among the resi-

dents of Saint Paul and Saint George. For all these reasons, I conclude that this is not an attractive approach to conducting the fur seal harvest.

State of Alaska

It is at least possible to think of the state of Alaska becoming an operating authority for the purpose of harvesting Pribilof fur seals. There is considerable interest in expanding the role of the state in managing marine mammals, and the Alaska Department of Fish and Game possesses a large fund of experience in the area of wildlife management. But the problems with this option are obvious and serious. The state of Alaska lacks the organizational capability to play the role of operating authority in contrast to manager with respect to the consumptive use of wild animals. It would take time to build up expertise and experience in this realm. And there is no reason to assume that the state government would be enthusiastic about moving in this direction in any case. In addition, the state of Alaska obviously would not wish to assume the other responsibilities of the Pribilof Islands Program. As a result, it would be necessary to negotiate a complex division of functions between the federal government and the state government regarding the management of the Pribilof Islands. In the final analysis, therefore, this arrangement would not only be likely to perpetuate many of the problems associated with federal management of the harvest, it would also introduce new complications relating to federal/state relations. In short, while it may be intriguing to think about creating a role for the state in conducting the Pribilof seal harvest, I cannot see any grounds for concluding that this is a serious option at this time.

Federal Government

No doubt the simplest way of resolving our problem would be to retain the existing arrangement. The federal government serves as an operating authority with a monopoly over the harvest of fur seals on the Pribilof Islands. The harvest is carried out as part of the Pribilof Islands Program, which in turn is under the administrative jurisdiction of the National Marine Fisheries Service. As I have already suggested, however, there are major problems with this arrangement. To begin with, the past record of the federal government as an operating authority for the seal harvest is not inspiring. If anything, conditions on the islands deteriorated following the takeover of the harvest by the federal government in 1910. Recently, the federal Court of Claims awarded the Aleut communities of Saint Paul and Saint George $8.5 million as compensation for the failure of the federal government to engage in "fair and honorable dealings" with them over the period between 1870 and 1946.[65] And the evidence accumulated by the Court in reaching this decision leaves little doubt that the government used its monopoly position to reduce the residents of these communities to a position of absolute dependence after 1910.[66] Under the circumstances, to say that Saint Paul and Saint George were traditionally run as company towns is an understatement.

Unquestionably, the record of the federal government in conducting the Pribilof seal harvest has improved substantially since the passage of the Fur Seal Act of 1966 and the Alaska Native Claims Settlement Act of 1971. Genuine efforts have been made to attend to the welfare of the communities, to encourage local autonomy, and to turn over more responsibilities to the people of the communities. Nevertheless, severe problems remain. The whole situation is somewhat anomalous since NMFS is not set up to serve as an operating authority much less to run entire communities. Consequently, the Pribilof Islands Program exists in something of a backwater unaffected either by effective pressures to pursue economic efficiency or by sophisticated thinking about community development. As a result, the seal harvest is not conducted in an economically efficient fashion. Partly, this is because the federal government has enjoyed monopoly status in this industry for so long and because efficiency is hard to achieve in public sector operations under the best of circumstances. In part, this inefficiency is deliberate and amounts to a de facto subsidy to the community of Saint Paul since a more efficient harvesting process would involve greater mechanization and a consequent loss of jobs in the fur seal industry.[67]

Though a case can be made for the importance of protecting jobs on Saint Paul, these observations point to a more fundamental problem with the current method of conducting the seal harvest. Despite real improvements since 1966, the communities of Saint Paul and especially Saint George remain heavily dependent on the federal government, and a strong undertone of paternalism continues to pervade relations between federal authorities and the communities. Until these communities achieve a greater measure of economic self-sufficiency, they will continue to exhibit many of the economic and social psychological characteristics of company towns and there will be strong pressures to continue de facto subsidies as well as more direct welfare programs. Once economic self-sufficiency is achieved, however, policies like conducting the seal harvest on an intentionally inefficient basis will be unjustifiable.[68] In my judgment, there are prospects of taking significant steps toward economic self-sufficiency in these communities in the near future, especially if Tanadgusix and Tanaq, the village corporations, can begin to operate effectively without falling under the influence of outside investors or corporate interests. But the point I want to stress here is that the federal government has not done much to promote economic self-sufficiency on the Pribilofs even in the relatively enlightened years since the passage of PL 89–702. This is painfully clear for Saint George, but the observation is applicable to Saint Paul as well. Promoting economic self-sufficiency requires more than turning over selected public functions to a local government and operating a single industry inefficiently to

preserve jobs. At a minimum, it requires highly sensitive
efforts to promote self-confidence and the development of
business acumen among local residents as well as sophisticated and coherent thinking about prospects for broadening
the economic base of the communities. While I certainly do
not wish to disparage improvements in the performance of
the federal government with respect to the conduct of the fur
seal harvest since 1966, this method of conducting the harvest
still leaves much to be desired.

Public Corporation

An interesting variation on the existing method of
conducting the fur seal harvest would be to create a public
corporation under relatively loose federal supervision to run
the operation. The idea would be to organize a kind of TVA
for the Pribilofs, which would conduct the fur seal harvest
and perhaps stimulate other forms of economic activity as
well. In comparison with the existing arrangement, a public
corporation would have several advantages. It would not
occupy an anomalous position in an agency with no other
operating functions. It would not be burdened with a history
of paternalism and insensitivity to local needs. And it would
have stronger incentives to pursue efficiency in the fur seal
industry together with alternative activities aimed at broadening the economic base of Saint Paul and Saint George. At
the same time, this option has serious drawbacks. The Pribilof situation is not as favorable as that originally presented to
the TVA. A public corporation for the Pribilofs could not
make money if it had to assume all the obligations currently
lodged in the Pribilof Islands Program. A decision to create a
public corporation for the fur seal harvest while retaining the
Pribilof Islands Program for other purposes, in contrast,
would generate severe bureaucratic complications and might
well lead to a situation in which Congress would be increasingly reluctant to appropriate funds to cover PL 89–702
obligations in the realms of health, welfare, and general

community support. Moreover, a public corporation of this type could hardly be counted on to become an effective promoter of self-confidence and autonomy among the residents of Saint Paul and Saint George. Of course, it is possible that local people would assume positions of leadership in the public corporation, acquiring business acumen and leadership experience in this fashion. It is more likely, however, that the public corporation would emerge as a competitor to Tanadgusix and Tanaq in the economic development of the Pribilofs. In my judgment, this would not be conducive to the growth of local self-confidence and autonomy, and, therefore, to the achievement of a more viable socioeconomic configuration for Saint Paul and Saint George during the foreseeable future. Overall, while a public corporation for the harvest of fur seals might well be an improvement over the existing arrangement, this option strikes me as far from ideal.

Village Corporations

A final alternative would be for the federal government to enter into contracts for the harvesting and processing of sealskins with Tanadgusix on Saint Paul and with Tanaq on Saint George in the event that the Saint George moratorium is lifted.[69] Tanadgusix and Tanaq are profit-making corporations mandated under the terms of section 8 of PL 92–203 and incorporated under the laws of the state of Alaska. Each corporation has been capitalized on the basis of payments received from the Alaska Native Fund; each is in the process of acquiring land both on the Pribilofs and on the Aleutian chain, and each has a strong interest in developing profitable business ventures.[70] From the point of view of the federal government, such an arrangement would be far more commonplace than the current arrangement for the Pribilof fur seal harvest. Many publicly owned or managed natural resources (for example, oil and gas, hard minerals, timber) are exploited on the basis of contracts or leases with private enterprises. While such contracts are sometimes allocated through a competitive bidding system, there is ample precedent for the type of administrative allocation that would be necessary in this case.[71] In fact, the federal government has already entered into an informal contract with Tanadgusix to handle the by-products of the sealing operation. There are numerous variations on this basic option, and the details of an actual agreement would have to be worked out with some care. My initial judgment, however, is that the preferred formula would be to negotiate fixed-term contracts with provisions for annual royalty payments to the federal government as well as for suspension or revocation designed to ensure compliance with environmental regulations.

The overwhelming virtue of this option is that it could be used to make a major contribution toward setting the communities of Saint Paul and Saint George on the road to economic self-sufficiency and sociopolitical independence. Every effort should be made to promote this outcome in working out the terms of the relevant contracts. The corporate leadership could be offered extensive but nonpaternalistic assistance in operating the industry during a transitional period. The proceeds from the harvest should go to the corporations, which could then pay royalties to the federal government.[72] Initially, these royalties might be kept at a modest level, since the corporations would want to operate the sealing industry on an efficient basis and this would generate a need for capital to initiate new economic activities to compensate for jobs lost in the sealing industry. Also, it would be necessary for the federal government to continue to fulfill its obligations toward Saint Paul and Saint George in the realms of health, welfare, and general community support, at least in the short run. Entering into contracts with Tanadgusix and Tanaq for the conduct of the fur seal harvest would hardly constitute an excuse to terminate all federal obligations to the Pribilof communities. Such a move would be a certain recipe for disaster. The basic objective of contracting out the seal harvest should be to move these communities toward economic self-sufficiency as well as sociopolitical autonomy. And this requires a careful transition to locally controlled industry of a productive but nondisruptive sort followed, in due course, by a gradual reduction of outside support for health, welfare, and general community operations.

This option for the conduct of the fur seal harvest is not without its own problems. To begin with, Tanadgusix and Tanaq do not have proven records. They have yet to demonstrate that they can achieve impressive business successes,[73] and they must overcome a certain air of skepticism as well as an exploitative attitude on the part of some outsiders. The federal government would have to take steps to ensure that environmental regulations aimed at safeguarding the seal herds and the surrounding ecosystem were respected under this arrangement. As I have already suggested, this might be accomplished by including provisions for suspension or revocation in the event of gross violations in the contracts with Tanadgusix and Tanaq. While there would be a need for continuous monitoring of compliance under this arrangement, this problem would be no more severe than it is in many other situations involving the use of natural resources. Beyond this, it would be necessary to alter several existing statutes to implement the arrangement under consideration here. Sections 104 and (probably) 101 of PL 89–702 would have to be amended to permit commercial harvesting of fur seals not under the direct control of the Secretary of Commerce. Further, section 6(e) of the Alaska Statehood Act as well as sections 407 and 408 of PL 89–702 should be changed to eliminate any state claims on the proceeds from the seal harvest. Presumably, this alteration would not arouse determined opposition. The state has not received payments under section 6(e) since 1969, and the justification for this provision is not compelling under current conditions in any case.[74] Statutory adjustments are seldom cut-and-dried, especially at the federal level. Nonetheless, it seems to me that the need for these adjustments should not be allowed to stand as a serious obstacle if the argument in favor of contracting the seal harvest to Tanadgusix and Tanaq is deemed persuasive on other grounds.

Where does this leave us with respect to the basic question concerning the preferred method of conducting the Pribilof seal harvest? In my judgment, there is much to be said for experimenting with the option of contracting with Tanadgusix and Tanaq to conduct the harvest. The only serious alternative is to retain a system in which the federal government serves as an operating authority. And as I have indicated, this option has severe flaws, at least as applied to the Pribilof Islands at this time. The proposal to enter into contracts with Tanadgusix and Tanaq is certainly not trouble free. Not surprisingly, proven business skills are in short supply in these communities, and the village corporations have yet to demonstrate their ability to conduct major business ventures successfully in a competitive wrold. Yet, it would be possible to experiment with this arrangement without endangering the Pribilof seal herds by insisting on appropriate provisions for suspension or revocation. There would be nothing irrevocable about the whole arrangement under consideration here. And above all, this option offers hope for the achievement of economic self-sufficiency for Saint Paul and Saint George without encouraging developments likely to transform these communities and to disrupt the surrounding ecosystem within ten to fifteen years. Admittedly, this plan is not likely to yield constructive results without an ample measure of sensitivity and good will on all sides. But I am convinced that it is worth a try.

CONCLUSION

The principal conclusions concerning public policy and the role of the state licensed by this analysis can be summarized quite simply. The commercial harvest of Pribilof fur seals should continue, albeit on a controlled basis to ensure the health and stability of the seal herds. The international regime for fur seals should be reconfirmed. To this end, it is desirable to extend the 1957 Convention. In the process, however, efforts should be made to renegotiate the Convention to introduce several specific changes. Maximum sustained yield (MSY) does not constitute a clear-cut guideline for the management of fur seals, and the Convention's preamble should probably be altered accordingly. The problem with the American-sponsored alternative to MSY, optimum sustained population (OSP), is that it has little analytic content and is subject to unrestrained political manipulation.[75] Therefore, it might be better to lay down more specific guidelines in this area, even while recognizing that political considerations will always be important in determining harvest levels. In addition, the Saint George moratorium should be lifted. Though this could be achieved through a decision of the Fur Seal Commission rather than any alteration of the Convention, an examination of this situation does suggest a desirable supplement to the language of the existing Convention. No doubt, there would be widespread opposition to giving local communities veto power over management decisions relating to fur seals. But there is a persuasive case to be made for including a provision in the revised Convention designed to compel the Commission to consider carefully the views of local residents before making decisions drastically affecting the interests of these communities.[76]

With respect to the conduct of the harvest, we should experiment with an arrangement whereby Tanadgusix and Tanaq undertake to conduct the harvest under contracts with the federal government. These contracts should contain effective provisions to ensure the continued health and stability of the Pribilof seal herds. The implementation of this arrangement would require suitable alterations in certain provisions of PL 89–702 and PL 85–508. Note, however, that it would not terminate all federal obligations spelled out in the provisions of PL 89–702, and it would not eliminate the role of the Pribilof Islands Program, at least during the near future. In fact, it would be critical for the federal government to effect this transition in a sensitive and supportive way, making every effort to maximize the chances of Tanadgusix and Tanaq succeeding in this venture. Only in this way can we hope to facilitate the achievement of economic self-sufficiency and sociopolitical independence for Saint Paul and Saint George during the foreseeable future.

Finally, this case study suggests several observations about the consumptive use of wild animals, especially under the supervision of the state. With all due respect to the philosophical precepts underlying preservationist views, the arguments in favor of consumptive use seem compelling under some conditions. Of course, this does not mean that consumptive use is always acceptable or that it should be approved casually or without careful assessment of the probable consequences in specific cases. On the contrary, I would argue that efforts to articulate arguments in opposition to consumptive use can be extremely useful, and I do not wish to be interpreted as condoning consumptive use on an indiscriminate basis. Nonetheless, it seems to me that the case for consumptive use of Pribilof fur seals is persuasive, at least under current conditions.

Four

Enforcing Public Regulations: The Fishery Conservation and Management Act of 1976

Much has been written about the efforts of states to regulate an ever-expanding range of activities both in the private sector and in the public sector.[1] The bulk of this literature, however, deals either with the choice of basic regulatory policies or with the formulation and promulgation of specific regulations. It has little to say about the problems of obtaining compliance with regulations following their promulgation. Policy choices and the formulation of regulations are obviously important. Nonetheless, they can do little to promote the goals of the state unless those subject to the resultant regulations generally comply with them. Consequently, there is a marked imbalance in our understanding of regulation. This chapter constitutes a small contribution toward rectifying this imbalance. It offers a detailed assessment of experience to date with efforts to enforce the network of regulations promulgated under the terms of the Fishery Conservation and Management Act of 1976 (PL 94–265, 90 Stat. 331, 16 USC 1801 et seq.).[2]

THE FCMA REGIME

In essence, the Fishery Conservation and Management Act (FCMA) sets up a regime of restricted common property for all marine fisheries under American control.[3] It makes no attempt to create exclusive rights in individual fish or stocks of fish. Rather, the Act outlines a structure of rules and institutions to govern the harvesting of fish. Specifically, the FCMA establishes a 200-mile fishery conservation zone (FCZ) contiguous to the baseline of the territorial sea of the United States (sec. 101) and asserts exclusive American authority to manage the fish stocks of the FCZ (sec. 102). Additionally, the Act outlines some general policies (for example, the pursuit of "optimum" yield) for the marine fisheries (sec. 301) and establishes an organizational structure to carry out these policies (secs. 302, 304). This new regime for the fisheries of the FCZ took effect on 1 March 1977. Not suprisingly, the entry into force of the FCMA has led to the formulation and promulgation of an array of specific regulations designed to transform the general provisions of the Act into behavioral prescriptions sufficiently detailed to guide the day-to-day behavior of individual fishermen and fishing vessels.[4]

Enforcement encompasses the use of sanctions on the part of a public authority for the purpose of obtaining compliance with behavioral prescriptions, whether or not they take the form of specific regulations. Enforcement is only one of the possible bases of compliance, and there is no a priori reason to assume that levels of compliance will invariably be low in the absence of enforcement efforts.[5] Thus, the actual level of compliance with fisheries regulations will be affected by several factors other than enforcement, such as the attitudes of the fishermen themselves, the incentives of individual firms or enterprises in the fishing industry, and the policies of the relevant government agencies. This means that in dealing with the general problem of compliance with FCMA regulations, it sometimes makes sense to pursue programs that have little to do with enforcement as such. To illustrate, there may be much to be said for efforts to socialize or educate the fishermen themselves or for programs designed to structure the incentives of individual firms in the fishing industry.

Nevertheless, there is general agreement among observers of marine fishing that these alternatives to enforcement cannot be counted on to produce high levels of compliance with fisheries regulations and that the development of an enforcement program is crucial to the effectiveness of any management regime for the marine fisheries. In part, this is attributable to the peculiar incentive structure associated with common property arrangements, even those featuring extensive sets of restrictions.[6] That there are no exclusive rights to stocks of fish inevitably gives each fisherman a distinct incentive to ignore regulations aimed at promoting conservation or economically efficient harvesting practices so long as he cannot be certain that others will comply with these regulations. Partly, the prospects for compliance in the absence of enforcement are undermined by the prospect of violating fisheries regulations in a manner that is not generally obvious to the outside world while the major fisheries involve large enough sums of money to offer a substantial temptation to violate or circumvent fisheries regulations. And these difficulties are only compounded when the fishermen are foreign nationals who may feel little sense of obligation to comply with regulations unilaterally promulgated by the American government. Moreover, the actual history of most marine fisheries offers no basis for optimism about the prospects of obtaining compliance with fisheries regulations on a voluntary basis. While there may well be variations among groups

of fishermen in this regard (for example, it is sometimes said
that Japanese fishermen are more "law abiding" than American fishermen), past experience surely supports the
argument of those who emphasize the importance of developing an enforcement program in conjunction with any
regime for the marine fisheries.[7]

The problem of enforcing FCMA regulations is addressed explicitly in sections 307 to 311 of PL 94-265, which
authorize agents of the Coast Guard and the National Marine
Fisheries Service (NMFS) to take a variety of steps to enforce
regulations promulgated under the Act. The core of the resultant program is a system of administrative sanctions involving
citations for minor infractions together with violations carrying relatively stiff monetary penalties—up to $25,000 per
infraction—for more serious infractions. In cases of gross
violation, authorized agents have the power to seize
offending vessels as well as the contents of their holds. These
civil actions can be supplemented with criminal arrests if any
attempt is made to resist or interfere with the enforcement
activities of authorized agents (sec. 309). To implement these
provisions of the FCMA, the Coast Guard and NMFS have
worked out an extensive set of enforcement routines. Legal
work arising in conjunction with enforcement incidents is
handled by the General Counsel's office of the National
Oceanic and Atmospheric Administration (NOAA) in cases
involving administrative sanctions and by the U.S. Attorney's
office for the relevant region in more serious cases.

To date, systematic enforcement activities carried out
under the authority of the FCMA have concentrated heavily,
though not exclusively, on the operations of foreign fishing
vessels (FFVs) in the fishery conservation zone.[8] A close reading of the FCMA (for example, sections 307 and 311) makes it
clear that the Act's enforcement provisions are aimed with
particular force at the operations of FFVs, though there is
nothing to prevent the enforcement of regulations directed to

domestic fishermen. American fishermen (with notable exceptions like tuna fishermen) have traditionally concentrated on inshore fisheries, which remain largely within the jurisdiction of individual states under the terms of the FCMA regime (sec. 306). The preliminary management plans, adopted at the outset to give the new regime substance right away, are directed primarily toward fisheries dominated by foreign fishing interests. The regional management councils set up by the FCMA (sec. 302) have experienced considerable delays in getting regular fishery management plans (FMPs) implemented. And they have often chosen, not surprisingly, to begin with individual fisheries featuring a heavy concentration of foreign entrants.[9] In addition, the political problems associated with efforts to enforce regulations on foreign fishermen are minor by comparison with those expected to arise when it comes to the enforcement of regulations on domestic fishermen in a systematic fashion. Though the relative emphasis should change over time, therefore, an evaluation of experience to date with the enforcement of regulations under the FCMA must be largely an analysis of efforts to enforce American fisheries regulations on foreign fishing vessels.

To lend substance to this study, I have chosen to approach the evaluation of enforcement activities under the FCMA through an intensive case study of the North Pacific region. As demarcated in section 302(a)(7) of the Act, this region encompasses "the fisheries in the Arctic Ocean, Bering Sea, and Pacific Ocean seaward of Alaska." The region covers an area of more than half a million square miles, a large domain for the enforcement of regulations by any standards.[10] While the fisheries of the North Pacific are among the richest in the world, they have been subjected to heavy usage raising serious conservation problems during recent years.[11] The Japanese and the Soviets have dominated the high seas fisheries of the region over the last twenty-five years, but South Korean, Taiwanese, Polish, and even Mexican fishermen have begun to show an interest in these fisheries during the 1970s. American fishermen, by contrast, have played only a minor role in the high seas fisheries of the North Pacific during the postwar period, though section 2(a)(7) of the FCMA specifically encourages an expansion of American efforts in these fisheries in the future.

THE RECORD

Some sense of the extent of the enforcement problem of the North Pacific can be obtained from an examination of the magnitude of foreign fishing operations in the region. Table 3 presents data on foreign fishing activities in the Bering Sea and the Gulf of Alaska, the major fishing grounds of the region. The unit of measure is the vessel day, a standard adopted recently in preference to the simpler notion of counting the number of vessels making an appearance on the fishing grounds during a given period because it conveys information about the intensity of fishing operations in the

TABLE 3
FOREIGN FISHING EFFORT OFF ALASKA
(IN VESSEL DAYS)

Month	1977	1978	1979
January	3,461	1,878	2,706
February	3,122	3,694	4,214
March	2,271	4,090	4,149
April	2,254	4,636	3,788
May	5,765	6,916	4,213
June	10,508	7,412	not available

SOURCE: U.S. Coast Guard, 17th District Headquarters (Juneau).

region. There are apt to be 200 to 300 foreign fishing vessels in the region at any one time during the high season. The principal fisheries of the North Pacific in which foreign vessels participate include the high seas salmon fishery, the herring fishery, fisheries for numerous demersal species (for example, pollock, flounders, pacific cod, sablefish, and rock fish), and fisheries for sedentary species like crabs and snails. These fisheries are not constant throughout the year. While table 3 does not give a complete picture, the months of May through August constitute the high season for fishing in the region. Fishing activities taper off substantially in the North Pacific during other months, though they do not come to a halt, as the table makes clear.

The Coast Guard compiles a daily Fleet Disposition Report (FDR) giving the last known location and activity of each fishing vessel in the North Pacific portion of the fishery conservation zone. These FDRs are assembled at the Coast Guard's 17th District Headquarters in Juneau from information transmitted by the fishing vessels themselves as well as field reports from all units participating in the Alaska Patrol (ALPAT). They are now put together by computer and distributed to individual ALPAT units by teletype. Since the summer of 1978, FDRs have been compiled and distributed to ALPAT units seven days a week. While this tool is not without its problems, the possession of an up-to-date FDR makes it possible for an ALPAT unit in the field to identify any fishing vessel encountered immediately upon contact and to run a preliminary check on such things as the date on which the vessel was last boarded.

The scale of the enforcement operation mounted by ALPAT emerges from the figures gathered in table 4. The phrase ''cutter patrol days'' refers to days actually under way on ALPAT missions in the North Pacific. Vessels employed on these missions are high endurance cutters (WHEC 378s), medium endurance cutters (WMEC 210s), and an occasional buoy tender. While on ALPAT missions, these vessels generally operate out of the Kodiak Support Center and are under the administrative control of the 17th District, though few of them are permanently based at Kodiak. At present, ALPAT makes use of vessels based in Long Beach, San Francisco, Seattle, and Honolulu as well as Kodiak. All boardings of foreign fishing vessels are carried out by boarding parties (ordinarily 5 to 6 men) from ALPAT cutters. NMFS agents now accompany approximately 30 percent of ALPAT surface missions. These agents typically participate in Coast Guard boarding parties, but they do not command these parties. ALPAT cutters have HH–52 helicopters deployed on some, but not all, missions. Aerial patrols are conducted by C–130 transports and HH–3 helicopters based at the Kodiak Air Station. These aircraft fly fixed ALPAT surveillance routes on a regular basis, though detailed schedules are not announced to prevent fishing vessels from obtaining advance knowledge of the pattern of ALPAT aerial patrols. At the beginning of the FCMA system, NMFS agents accompanied most aerial patrols, but the ratio seems to have declined sharply more recently. The prime function of the aerial patrols is to supply information for the FDRs. But they are also capable of detecting violations of geographical closing lines, seasonal restrictions, and procedural regulations (for example, failure to display an international radio call sign properly).

It is worth noting that the Alaska Patrol did not originate with the passage of the FCMA. The Coast Guard had mounted ALPAT missions for some years before 1977 in conjunction with the International Pacific Halibut Convention, the International North Pacific Fisheries Convention, and various bilateral agreements with Japan, Canada, the Soviet Union, and Korea.[12] Nevertheless, the passage of the FCMA led to a significant increase in ALPAT effort: an additional high endurance cutter and several additional aircraft have been added to the patrol, and information processing capabilities at District Headquarters in Juneau have been

TABLE 4
COAST GUARD PATROL EFFORT—1977–1979

Month	Cutter patrol days	Aircraft patrol hours	Aircraft miles flown	JA	KS	PL	TW	UR	MX	Tot.
1977										
March	100	155.3	24,650							152
April	84	153.5	22,753							136
May	81	179.0	23,564							164
June	132	170.4	21,889							382
July	101	215.7	31,328	728	27	1	0	12		768
August	58	192.2	36,394	558	33	0	12	17		610
September	89	171.3	35,678	903	39	0	2	6		1009
October	84	102.3	28,714	328	59	1	0	88		476
November	73	170.7	38,595	245	50	6	1	89		391
December	45	121.7	29,118	127	8	0	2	71		208
1978										
January	45	119.4	30,629	65	1	0	0	59		125
February	75	105.0	32,546	310	9	0	3	166		488
March	76	138.8	43,905	315	42	0	1	202		560
April	73	115.4	30,367	293	30	0	5	88		416
May	59	189.7	28,054	176	43	0	0	36		315
June	102	301.7	57,219	338	52	0	0	40		442
July	data missing owing to computer problem									
August	137	474.6	16,042	663	72	0	3	1		739
September	67	188.0	46,926	401	58	0	7	175		641
October	53	88.9	31,754	311	47	0	2	51		411
November	96	117.3	38,955	485	57	8	2	99		651
December	38	116.0	18,904	225	19	0	0	57		301
1979										
January	32	67.0	29,848	161	58	0	3	31	0	255
February	25	128.0	16,920	320	24	0	6	57	2	409
March	31	176.0	24,071	257	31	3	4	77	8	380
April	53	170.0	32,044	448	73	22	4	19	0	566
May	93	162.0	27,440	514	72	23	6	8	2	625
June (1-24)	70	107.0	17,390	523	85	19	0	36	7	670

ABBREVIATIONS: JA = Japan; KS = Korea; PL = Poland; TW = Taiwan; UR = Soviet Union; MX = Mexico.

SOURCE: U.S. Coast Guard, 17th District Headquarters (Juneau).

expanded substantially. According to one authoritative estimate, enforcement efforts have been increased by about one third compared with the pre-FCMA level.[13] Turn now to some indicators of the performance of ALPAT. Under FCMA regulations, foreign fishing vessels are required to check into the fishery conservation zone (FCZ), to signal changes of fishing area within the zone, and to check out upon leaving the FCZ. Nonetheless, ALPAT conducts a surveillance operation to keep track of foreign fishing vessels on the North Pacific fishing grounds on a regular basis. Much of this operation is the responsibility of the aerial patrols, though surface units also file daily reports on all vessels contacted in the course of their patrols. The nominal goal is to sight 90 percent of the foreign fishing vessels actually on the grounds during each two week period.

Table 5 summarizes the results of this surveillance program for the North Pacific region. The term "fishing vessels" refers here to independent vessels and excludes catcher boats or dependent vessels operating with mother ships. It is apparent that the operation has generally failed to reach the 90 percent goal, though actual sightings have approached this level with some frequency. The success of this component of ALPAT is highly sensitive to competition from other Coast Guard activities (for example, search and rescue [SAR] missions) as well as weather conditions, especially in the Bering Sea, which frequently make it difficult to obtain visual identifications of individual vessels.

The key element in the enforcement program currently mounted by ALPAT is a continuing series of boardings and site inspections. The general goal is to board each foreign fishing vessel on the grounds on an average of once every ninety days. Table 6 presents data both on the number of boardings conducted and on the proportion of these boardings leading to enforcement incidents. The phrase "enforcement incidents" covers all citations, violations, and seizures. The standards applicable to these incidents are the Foreign

TABLE 5
SURVEILLANCE STANDARD ANALYSIS

Time period	Number of FFVs on grounds*	Number of FFVs sighted during period*	Percent sighted
1977			
October	175	144	82.3
November	142	113	79.6
December	64	49	76.6
1978			
January	33	19	57.6
February	62	45	72.6
March	47	44	93.4
April	63	55	87.3
May	130	100	76.9
June	227	148	65.2
July	285	214	75.1
August	245	142	58.0
September	269	208	77.3
October	264	178	67.4
November	242	205	84.7
December	116	81	69.8
1979			
January	161	155	96.3
February	277	257	92.8
March	218	162	74.3
April	215	185	86.1
May	240	195	81.3

*The method of computation for this table allows an individual vessel to be counted more than once in the same month. Therefore, the table cannot be used to estimate the level of foreign fishing effort in the North Pacific sector of the fishery conservation zone.

SOURCE: U.S. Coast Guard, 17th District Headquarters (Juneau).

TABLE 6

BOARDINGS AND ENFORCEMENT INCIDENTS

(INCIDENTS/BOARDINGS)

Month	Japan	USSR	Korea	Poland	Taiwan	Mexico	All	Percent resulting in incidents
1977								
March	1/26	4/21	1/1	N/A	N/A		6/48	12.5
April	6/38	2/9	0/4	N/A	N/A		8/61	13.1
May	2/72	0/18	0/1	N/A	N/A		2/94	02.1
June	6/171	0/3	0/0	N/A	0/0		6/174	03.5
July	2/73	0/4	5/12	N/A	N/A		7/89	07.8
August	9/52	0/2	1/4	N/A	4/4		14/62	22.6
September	3/65	0/12	1/6	N/A	1/1		5/84	06.0
October	0/20	0/6	3/10	0/0	N/A		3/36	08.3
November	0/22	0/12	0/3	0/1	0/0		0/38	00.0
December	1/16	1/13	0/1	N/A	N/A		2/30	06.8
ALL 1977	30/555	7/100	11/42	0/1	5/5		53/716	07.4
1978								
January	0/5	0/0	N/A	N/A	N/A		0/5	00.0
February	7/20	7/18	0/0	N/A	0/0		14/41	34.2
March	1/20	3/26	0/3	N/A	0/0		4/45	08.9

April	4/46	0/23	1/4	N/A	3/3	8/76	10.5
May	8/47	8/22	1/9	N/A	0/0	17/79	21.5
June	3/33	3/4	0/5	N/A	0/0	6/42	14.3
July	12/68	0/0	0/6	N/A	0/0	12/72	16.2
August	6/29	0/0	1/5	N/A	0/0	7/34	20.6
September	2/36	6/25	2/5	N/A	0/1	10/67	15.0
October	0/17	1/3	0/6	N/A	0/0	1/26	03.9
November	3/35	3/14	3/11	0/0	0/0	9/60	15.0
December	1/30	2/9	0/1	0/0	0/0	3/40	07.5
ALL 1978	47/386	33/144	8/55	0/0	3/4	96/589	16.3
1979							
January	1/4	0/0	1/7	0/0	0/0	2/11	18.2
February	1/6	0/6	1/2	0/0	0/1	2/15	13.3
March	1/2	1/6	0/0	0/0	1/2	3/10	30.0
April	1/17	0/1	0/7	0/2	0/0	1/27	03.7
May	2/35	0/3	0/6	1/1	0/0	3/45	06.7
1979 so far	6/64	1/16	2/22	1/3	1/2	11/108	10.2

SOURCE: U.S. Coast Guard, 17th District Headquarters (Juneau).

Fishing Regulations promulgated in the U.S. Federal Register and published in the *Code of Federal Regulations* (50 CFR 611). Operators of all foreign fishing vessels are expected to possess up-to-date knowledge of the precise content of these regulations.[14] Initial decisions about the application of the regulations to individual cases are made by the captain of the ALPAT cutter on the scene, acting on information obtained by the relevant boarding party. In ambiguous cases, the captain may initiate a radio consultation with 17th District Headquarters before making a definite decision. Whenever a seizure is contemplated, it is necessary to obtain permission to go ahead from Washington as well as from the 17th District in Juneau.

A more detailed breakdown of enforcement incidents in the North Pacific for the period beginning 1 March 1977 appears in Table 7. Citations are roughly equivalent to warnings issued in conjunction with traffic infractions; they are explicitly authorized under section 311(c) of the FCMA. They carry no monetary penalties, but all citations are noted on the fishing permits of the vessels involved and a record of their issuance is kept. Violations are civil offenses and ordinarily result in penalties. Under the terms of section 308(a), these penalties are not to exceed $25,000 for each violation. A fishing vessel and its catch are subject to seizure for more severe infractions of FCMA regulations (sec. 310). While a vessel taken into custody may be subject to civil forfeiture, the standard practice to date has been to release seized vessels upon payment of relatively large penalties. The exact boundaries among these types of infractions are somewhat ambiguous and subject to interpretation on a case-by-case basis. As the data in table 7 indicate, seizures were uncommon in the North Pacific before 1979: only two such cases occurred in the region between 1 March 1977 and 31 December 1978. But there has been a sharp increase in the frequency of seizures during 1979—there were four during the first six months of the year. Beyond this, individuals can be charged with criminal offenses under the terms of section 309

TABLE 7
ENFORCEMENT ACTIONS

Time period	Citations	Violations	Seizures
1977			
March	2	4	
April	8[a]	1	
May	1	1	
June	4	2	
July	6	1	
August	8	6[b]	
September	5[c]	1	1
October	5	2[d]	
November	1		
December	3[e]		
ALL 1977	43	18	1
1978			
January	4		
February	14	2	1
March	4[f]	1	
April	8	1	
May	16	6	
June	3	2	
July	14	2	
August	4		
September	8	2	
October	1		
November	2	1	
December	1		
ALL 1978	79	17	1
1979			
January		1	1
February		1	1
March	2	1	
April	1		
1979 so far	3	3	2[g]

[a]One upgraded to a violation   [d]One dismissed
[b]Three downgraded to citations   [e]One dismissed
[c]One dismissed   [f]One cancelled
[g]Two additional seizures occurred in June 1979

SOURCE: U.S. Coast Guard, 17th District Headquarters (Juneau).

of the FCMA. These offenses would ordinarily involve such things as refusing to receive an authorized boarding party or interfering with the efforts of a boarding party to carry out its inspection (see sec. 307 of the FCMA for details). To date, no criminal charges under section 309 have been preferred with respect to foreign fishing operations in the North Pacific.

How are enforcement incidents handled once the ALPAT documentation is assembled and forwarded to NMFS? There are two distinct tracks for the disposition of these cases. All situations involving citations and violations are handled through administrative law procedures supervised by National Oceanic and Atmospheric Administration (NOAA) attorneys. These procedures have formal provisions for appeals, and they can lead to proceedings in federal district court. In practice, however, they typically eventuate in bargaining and the negotiation of settlements on a case-by-case basis. In the North Pacific, section 308 penalties for violations have been running in the range of $2,500 to $10,000, and there is no evidence of any sharp trend in the magnitude of these penalties. The administrative law procedures under discussion here were originally centralized in Washington, but they have now been decentralized to the regional offices of NOAA (at Juneau for cases in the North Pacific region). This shift was a response to complaints about slowness and lack of detailed knowledge of individual cases on the part of Washington officials, and it appears to have resulted in noticeable improvements since taking effect in the middle of 1978.[15]

Infractions leading to seizures or criminal charges go directly to the office of the U.S. Attorney for the relevant region (at Anchorage in this instance). Here, too, the prevailing legal arrangements have led to extensive bargaining. Before 1979, when seizures were uncommon, individual cases were settled with the vessel and its catch being released in return for the payment of a relatively large penalty ($335,000 for the 1977 case and $200,000 for the 1978 case). The upsurge of seizures during 1979, however, has led to a new era in the handling of serious fisheries cases, and several issues relating to these infractions are now in the process of being formally resolved by the federal courts. The U.S. Attorney's office, for its part, has moved to sell catches of seized vessels at auction and to raise penalties, and it is contemplating instituting civil forfeiture proceedings against offending vessels themselves. At the same time, attorneys for the fishermen have raised important questions about possible fourth and fifth amendment violations in conjunction with ALPAT operations and have pointed to the lack of clear-cut standards for the computation of penalties in individual cases. No doubt these formal actions will have a salutory effect in the sense that they will provide authoritative interpretations for complex FCMA regulations and generate precedents to guide the handling of future cases. Nevertheless, the current situation with respect to the disposition of cases involving serious infractions of FCMA regulations is cloudy at best.

EFFECTIVENESS

Unquestionably, the central problem in evaluating any enforcement program is to devise some measure of its effectiveness.[16] In this respect, fisheries regulations certainly do not constitute an exception. Accordingly, the following questions come into focus. How successful is ALPAT in deterring FCMA infractions that would occur in its absence? What proportion of those who in fact violate ALPAT regulations in the North Pacific are apprehended by ALPAT? Note that the problem here is to assess the effectiveness of this enforcement program in the light of actual occurrences. It is not simply a matter of projecting expected levels of compliance on the basis of some initial assumptions about the behavior of fishermen and enforcement agents.[17]

In principle, it is possible to approach the measurement of efffectiveness directly. Thus, let x be the level of violations that would occur in the absence of ALPAT and y be the level of unsuppressed infractions given the existing ALPAT enforcement program. Then we can write

$$E = 1 - \frac{y}{x}$$

where E is an index of effectiveness. The larger the value of E, the greater the effectiveness of ALPAT in enforcing fisheries regulations.

It turns out, however, that there are severe practical problems impeding efforts to compute values for both x and y under real-world conditions. Consider first the situation with respect to x. There is no good methodology for calculating this element of the index. In the absence of an enforcement program, it is not possible to monitor activities in the high seas fisheries with any accuracy.[18] By definition, the introduction of some enforcement operation, if only for purposes of surveillance, would alter the situation in such a way as to make x irrelevant. Beyond this, opinions or subjective estimates vary widely concerning the putative value of x. Some believe that all fishermen will violate regulations if given a chance, while others assume that fishermen are generally law-abiding entrepreneurs who can be expected to comply with many, if not most, regulations on a voluntary basis. Unfortunately, all of these judgments appear to stem more from the personality of the estimator than from any profound knowledge of existential reality. As I indicated in the introduction to this chapter, there are reasons to expect violations of fisheries regulations to be relatively high in the absence of enforcement. These have to do with such things as the nature of common property arrangements and the feasibility of clandestine violations. But these general propositions are surely insufficient to allow the computation of specific values for x. They can do no more than indicate tendencies, and in any case they may be offset in specific situations by countervailing forces like efforts to socialize fishermen regarding regulations or the nature of the command structure within individual fishing companies.

The situation with respect to the computation of values for y is much the same. To the extent that violations are not detected by the enforcement program associated with a system of regulations, it follows that we can have no direct knowledge of their occurrence. No doubt, there may be indirect hints concerning infractions, such as reports from private parties or the appearance of damaged fish in closed areas. And those involved in the enforcement operation are seldom without opinions relating to the extent and magnitude of violations going undetected. But all these sources of evidence are highly unsatisfactory, at least in the case of the marine fisheries of the North Pacific. In such a vast region, it is relatively easy to violate specific regulations out of sight of any onlookers, and opinions concerning this issue once again vary on the basis of personal world view at least as much as on the basis of pertinent evidence. Therefore, E is an index that is as hard to use to good effect in practice as it is simple and straightforward in principle.

Of course, it would be nice to have a continuous measure of effectiveness rather than a snapshot index of the type discussed above. Ideally, this would take the form of a production function for E as exemplified in figure 3. Such a function would indicate the results in terms of the suppression of violations which would flow from any given level of effort in the enforcement program. It is obvious, however, that it is impossible to construct an empirically based function of this sort for the case of fisheries regulations. My discussion of the problems of computing values for x and y makes it clear that it is not feasible to establish even a single point on such a production function with confidence. Further, we do not have numerous cases from which to draw inferences concerning the probable shape of this function, and serious experimentation is out of the question in this realm. Nonetheless, I think there are good reasons to assume that this function will exhibit certain general characteristics, which are of some importance in contemplating the enforcement of fisheries regulations. Thus, enforcement programs

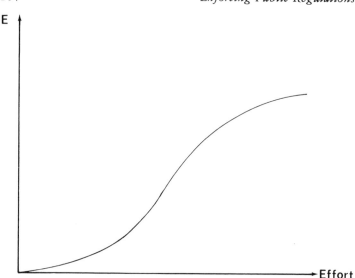

Fig. 3. Effectiveness of enforcement operations (*E*) as a function of effort.

are apt to encounter an initial lumpiness in the sense that there is a threshold of effort that must be reached before any program has significant effects in reducing the level of violations. We can expect declining marginal productivity to set in as enforcement programs become larger and larger. Moreover, the production function for enforcement can be expected to level off completely at some point, as illustrated in figure 3. This implies that it will never be possible to eliminate all violations of fisheries regulations and that it would be irrational for a public authority to pursue perfect compliance as a goal. These characteristics are reflected in the production function portrayed in figure 3.

Given all these problems plaguing attempts to measure effectiveness directly, it is hardly surprising that there is a lively interest in the development of indirect approaches to the measurement of effectiveness. In fact, several indirect approaches are possible in connection with the evaluation of enforcement programs for fisheries regulations. Perhaps the most interesting of these indirect approaches focuses on trends in the ratio of enforcement incidents to boardings (i/b) over time. There is a plausible rationale for this measure. Assume that ALPAT boardings occur on a random basis as far as the fishing fleet is concerned and that for all practical purposes individual boardings are unannounced. It will then be the case that vessels actually boarded can be regarded as constituting a representative sample of the entire set of fishing vessels on the grounds. Assume further that boardings are carried out in a standardized fashion and that what is treated as an infraction in one case is interpreted as an infraction in other cases as well. Under these conditions, the ratio i/b, and especially trends in this ratio, can be employed to good advantage in evaluating the effectiveness of the enforcement program. A high value for i/b would license the conclusion that many violations of FCMA regulations are going undeterred and undetected. A declining ratio, by contrast, could be taken as evidence that the enforcement program was improving with respect to effectiveness. It is true that these interpretations are not logically entailed in any strict sense by the line of reasoning sketched here. All the same, they would have considerable credibility as appropriate inferences to be drawn from such observations.

It follows that it is worth computing and tracing the value of i/b over time for the North Pacific region. Figures 4 and 5 display the results of these computations for the period since the implementation of the FCMA on 1 March 1977. In general, these results are disappointing, at least from the point of view of reaching definite conclusions about the effectiveness of ALPAT. The most striking feature of these figures is the extent to which they portray fluctuations in the relationship between enforcement incidents and boardings in the North Pacific region. On the basis of this evidence, it is hard to draw any conclusions about the effectiveness of ALPAT. If

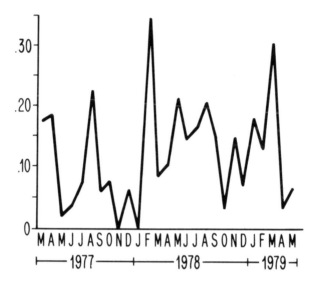

Fig. 4. Percent boardings resulting in enforcement incidents—all FFVs.

anything, there has been some tendency for *i/b* to rise, at least in the aggregate, over time. While this might be attributed to a growing sophistication in uncovering violations during individual boardings, the larger implications of this trend can hardly be a source of comfort for those concerned with the overall effectiveness of the enforcement program.

There are various possible explanations of these findings. Above all, there are good reasons to question the reasonableness of the assumptions underlying this indirect approach to measuring the effectiveness of the enforcement program for the North Pacific. For example, there are clear indications

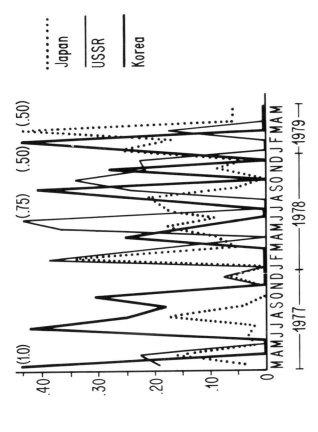

Percent boardings resulting in enforcement incidents—by nationality.

that boardings in this region have not followed a standardized pattern over the period since 1 March 1977. Particularly in the profiles of individual nationalities—see figure 5—monthly readings often rest on very small numbers of cases so that they may have little significance. It is possible that efforts on the part of fishermen to violate FCMA regulations are becoming more common as the fishermen acquire more intimate knowledge both of the regulations themselves and of possible methods of circumventing them. And as I suggested above, the enforcers may be acquiring increased sophistication in detecting infractions or devising successful tactics in their pursuit of violators. Whichever of these factors or combination of factors best accounts for the fluctuations displayed in figures 4 and 5, however, the i/b ratio cannot be regarded, at least at this stage, as offering much help in solving the problem of measuring the effectiveness of ALPAT.

An alternative indirect approach to effectiveness focuses on the condition of the pertinent stocks of fish rather than on specific enforcement efforts as such. After all, the fundamental management goal of the FCMA regime is presumably to maintain healthy fish stocks and to facilitate the recovery of stocks severely depleted under the preceding unrestricted common property arrangement. The pursuit of actual or potential violators is hardly an end in itself. Under the circumstances, we might focus on trends in the condition of the relevant fish stocks in attempting to resolve the effectiveness problem in evaluating enforcement programs in the realm of fisheries regulations. To the extent that these stocks are recovering nicely or remaining in a healthy state, we could simply assume that the enforcement program is operating effectively.

This alternative, however, leaves a great deal to be desired as an approach to the effectiveness problem. Above all, the logical links between the condition of the relevant stocks and the effectiveness of ALPAT are tenuous at best. Individual stocks could decline dramatically even in the presence of a supremely effective enforcement program. This could occur, for example, if the North Pacific Fisheries Management Council set inappropriate total allowable catch levels (TACs) year after year or if the regulations promulgated under the FCMA proved defective for the conditions encountered in the North Pacific region.[19] By the same token, improvements in stock conditions could certainly occur even in the face of relatively extensive violations of FCMA regulations. While the study of population dynamics leaves many questions unanswered in the marine fisheries, it does not take any profound knowledge to see that some of the existing FCMA regulations have little bearing on the condition of individual stocks of fish in the FCZ. Therefore, this indirect approach to the effectiveness problem suffers from extreme tenuousness regarding the links between the indicator proposed and the underlying issue under consideration.

In any event, assessing the condition of individual stocks of fish turns out to be about as difficult as measuring the effectiveness of an enforcement program.[20] There are extensive unresolved theoretical problems in this area, especially when an ecosystem supports numerous interdependent species as it does in the North Pacific. Data problems loom large in this field, and there are many North Pacific species (for example, squid and even herring) about whose population dynamics remarkably little is known. Further, the elapsed time between the inception of the FCMA regulations in 1977 and the present is so short that any responsible observer would be reluctant to hazard strong statements relating the introduction of the FCMA regime to the changing conditions of individual fish stocks. The study of stock conditions and of population dynamics more generally is of fundamental importance in conjunction with fisheries management. But I can see nothing but trouble resulting from attempts to make use of information concerning trends in stock conditions as an indirect approach to measuring the effectiveness of ALPAT.

All this leaves us with an obvious and important dilemma relating to the effectiveness of enforcement programs designed to obtain compliance with fisheries regulations. There are fundamental flaws both in direct approaches to the measurement of effectiveness and in indirect approaches to this problem. Yet effectiveness can hardly be ignored as a key issue in the evaluation of any enforcement program. I cannot provide a satisfactory solution to this problem; I do not even see the precise form that such a solution might take. Nevertheless, I do want to offer my own judgments concerning the effectiveness of the enforcement program for the North Pacific region. These judgments are clearly of a subjective character. But my experience with this enforcement program is relatively extensive; I have no personal interests to protect in this realm, and my training as a social scientist at least ensures that my judgments rest on systematic observations.[21]

At the outset, I would argue that it is impossible to construct overall generalizations about the effectiveness of ALPAT. I am certain that there is considerable variation in the effectiveness of ALPAT by type of violation. In my judgment, this is the most important dimension of variation associated with this enforcement program, though there is reason to believe that variations by type of fishing and by season of the year may also occur. Accordingly, I have attempted to categorize the fisheries regulations pertaining to the North Pacific into differentiable groups and to construct an estimate of ALPAT effectiveness for each of these groups. The results are displayed in table 8. Roughly speaking, this table proceeds from infractions that are of relatively minor significance to those that raise more basic questions about the fundamental management objectives associated with the FCMA regime. While I have no doubt that there is room for disagreement about the details of this classification, I feel confident that the central distinctions on which it rests are sound.

Several interpretive observations emerge from an examination of this table. There are some cases (for example, proper procedures) with respect to which infractions occurred with considerable frequency during the early months of the FCMA, declining substantially with the passage of time.

TABLE 8
ESTIMATED EFFECTIVENESS
(BY TYPE OF REGULATION)

Type of regulation *	Infractions without ALPAT	Infractions with ALPAT
1. permits (e.g. possession, proper display)	medium	low/negligible
2. proper procedures (e.g. check in/out, IRCSs, day shapes)	high	low
3. cooperativeness (e.g. resistance, facilitating boarding)	N/A	negligible
4. gear restrictions (e.g. longline hooks)	medium	low
5. seasons/time limits (e.g. opening and closing dates)	medium	low
6. area restrictions (e.g. three-mile limit, loading zones)	high/medium	low
7. prohibited or nontargeted species (e.g. retention, proper return to the sea)	high	medium
8. log/record keeping (e.g. misrepresentation, underlogging)	high	medium
9. national quotas— TALFFs by country (e.g. reporting weekly catch data)	high	medium

Scale
1. high
2. medium
3. low
4. negligible
5. N/A = not applicable

*Roughly speaking, these categories of regulations proceed from those that are of relatively minor significance to those that raise more basic questions about the fundamental management objectives associated with the FCMA regime.

Thus, it is no longer common to find foreign fishing vessels failing to display proper international radio call signs (IRCSs), provide adequate boarding ladders, fly day shapes while fishing, and so forth. There can be no doubt that this is substantially attributable to ALPAT enforcement operations and that it is a mark of the effectiveness of ALPAT, at least in this realm. Overall, however, my estimates suggest that ALPAT has compiled a mixed record with regard to effectiveness. As the table implies, there can be no doubt that ALPAT has cut back on the level of FCMA violations that would have occurred in the absence of a significant enforcement program. But by the same token, there are compelling reasons to conclude that ALPAT has not succeeded in reducing a number of types of violations to a negligible or low level. Whether marginal increases in the level of effectiveness in these areas could be obtained without incurring excessive costs is an issue to which I return in the next section of this chapter.

For the moment, I want to comment instead on the apparent inverse correlation between the level of ALPAT effectiveness and the seriousness of the violations in question. It turns out that those types of violations that are most likely to undermine the achievement of the fundamental objectives of the FCMA regime (for example, handling of prohibited species and proper log keeping) are the hardest to control on the basis of the existing enforcement program for the North Pacific. If this is intrinsic to the problem of enforcing fisheries regulations and not merely an artifact of the existing enforcement program, it raises important questions about the general prospects of the FCMA as a management scheme or regulatory system. Additionally, if this sort of situation is common in conjunction with many regulatory systems, as I suspect it is, the findings of this study concerning the problem of effectiveness suggest an issue that should be placed prominently on the agenda of future research dealing with the topic of regulation in general.

In the end, there is no escaping the fact that we must live with highly imperfect information concerning the effectiveness of efforts to enforce fisheries regulations. In the case of the North Pacific, this has led to several interesting developments, which undoubtedly have parallels in other regulatory programs. Above all, there is an inevitable tendency to fix on various surrogate indicators of performance in evaluating or justifying the activities of the enforcement program.[22] The most obvious surrogates in conjunction with ALPAT include measures of patrol effort, the frequency and intensity of enforcement boardings, and the frequency and severity of enforcement incidents. Each of these measures can be quantified with relative ease and presented in such a way as to emphasize the sustained effort being made, regardless of its ultimate effectiveness. Further, several of these measures are capable of producing dramatic effects when handled properly in public. For example, there is a certain drama associated with the seizure of a foreign vessel on the high seas, which can be played upon to convey to the public the sense that enforcement officers are making a concerted effort to apprehend violators of fisheries regulations.

Under the circumstances, it is easy enough to understand the motives of those who fix on these surrogate indicators of performance. Nevertheless, not only do these indicators bear no logical relationship to effectiveness as such, but it is also easy to show that significant dangers are associated with these practices. Concentrating on patrol effort may lead to unnecessary expenditures of resources on enforcement operations. A propensity to conduct frequent boardings to convey an appearance of effectiveness can lead to undue harrassment of fishermen and raise profound questions concerning the maintenance of constitutionally protected rights. And while seizures offer a showy public spectacle, they are costly in other respects. They take ALPAT units away from regular patrol duties for long periods; they are apt to lead to protracted and expensive litigation, and they are extremely costly from the point of view of affected fishermen and vessel owners quite apart from the formal penalties ultimately levied. Therefore, though the attractiveness of these surrogate indicators to enforcement personnel is understandable, there are compelling reasons to be cautious about their use from the perspective of sound management practices.

The inability to arrive at clear-cut measures of effectiveness also makes enforcement programs vulnerable to the impact of political pressures and ideological preferences. Since it is hard to assess the implications for effectiveness of different enforcement strategies or procedures, it is relatively easy for interested parties to push the adoption of alternative enforcement programs for other reasons. Sometimes this is a matter of bureaucratic politics, since the character of an enforcement program will often affect the extent to which it falls under the operational control of one agency or another (for example, Coast Guard or NMFS). In other cases, the motivation is simple economic interest arising when alternative enforcement programs do not lead to identical treatment for all types of violations. Or the problem may be explicitly ideological, as in cases where certain enforcement procedures are opposed by those concerned with the protection of civil liberties or with the avoidance of public sector interference in the activities of private enterprises.

This set of conditions is also apt to introduce a distinct element of volatility into the development and operation of an enforcement program. There are often pressures to reform an existing enforcement program, making more or less drastic changes in its mode of operation, and it is hard to evaluate existing arrangements or to assess proposed alternatives in terms of their implications for effectiveness. The result is typically a succession of politically inspired arrangements, none of which remains in place long enough to accumulate a substantial record of performance. To the best of my knowledge, this phenomenon is in no way peculiar to ALPAT or even to the realm of fisheries management. On the contrary, my impression is that the pattern is widespread, afflicting efforts to achieve compliance with systems or regulations in numerous substantive fields.

EFFICIENCY

Turn now to the question of efficiency. Is the basic character and magnitude of the enforcement program which has emerged under the FCMA regime about right? More specifically, do the gains attributable to these enforcement efforts outweigh the costs of the program? Could we obtain at a lower cost equally good results from the point of view of suppressing violations? Are there other, fundamentally different, enforcement strategies that might be preferable to the strategies employed by the existing enforcement program? Though the assessment of effectiveness constitutes the classic problem in evaluating enforcement programs, these questions about efficiency are obviously of great importance.

Virtually all attempts to think about efficiency systematically rest on utilitarian premises.[23] Among other things, this means we must make an effort to measure the costs and benefits associated with the enforcement of fisheries regulations. What does it cost to obtain compliance with FCMA regulations in the North Pacific? What are the benefits of deterring or apprehending violations of these regulations? Others have already considered the methodological problems arising in connection with these cost and benefit calculations and explored alternative approaches to measurement in this realm.[24] Accordingly, I shall not simply repeat the observations made in these prior discussions. But I do want to raise some basic questions about the computation of costs and benefits in this area and to comment on the computations offered in previous studies.[25]

The first thing to notice about the costs of enforcing FCMA regulations in the North Pacific is that there are several fundamentally different ways to conceptualize these costs and that the cost figures obtained vary widely depending upon which approach is taken. Thus, some may regard the enforcement operations of ALPAT as externalities or by-products of activites undertaken for other purposes. If the Coast Guard can justify the maintenance of extensive capabilities in conjunction with its military preparedness and search and rescue (SAR) missions, then the enforcement of fisheries regulations can be achieved in the course of exercising forces kept in being for other purposes. Alternatively, we may wish to focus on the increment to preexisting capabilities necessitated by the introduction of the FCMA regulations on 1 March 1977. As indicated above, ALPAT existed before the passage of the FCMA and fisheries law enforcement was not a novel undertaking in the spring of 1977. In fact, the federal government estimates that "The 1976 (pre-FCMA) level of fisheries law enforcement effort accomplished 75% of the desired level of FCMA enforcement."[26] Starting from this perspective, we might wish to concentrate on measuring the increment in enforcement costs occasioned by the implementation of the FCMA. Yet another approach is simply to focus on the operating and fixed costs of deploying all units that participate in the enforcement of fisheries regulations in the North Pacific. Thus, a cutter day under way on ALPAT would be attributed to the FCMA enforcement program regardless of any other justification for the existence of the unit, and all activities of the U.S. Attorney's office in Anchorage pertaining to fisheries cases would be placed on the account of the enforcement program whether or not the office would be maintained in any case for other purposes. It is obvious that this latter approach to calculating the costs of enforcing fisheries regulations will lead to far larger figures than either of the other procedures mentioned.

Nevertheless, let me proceed with the third option outlined above. It is always possible to discount the cost figures obtained in this way to adjust for the other two factors, whereas there is no straightforward way to move from the first or second option to the third. The first thing that becomes apparent in this connection is that there are numerous technical problems in computing the costs incurred by the Coast Guard in operating ALPAT. Above all, the Coast Guard organizes most of its accounting by district or geographical region rather than by mission or function. As a result, it is hard to separate out the costs of fisheries law enforcement from the costs attributable to other Coast Guard missions. In the case of ALPAT, this difficulty is compounded by the participation of units from five different Coast Guard districts in the FCMA enforcement program for the North Pacific. This leads to a variety of problems such as deciding how to allocate the costs incurred when a cutter steams from, say, Honolulu to Kodiak to move into position to proceed on an ALPAT mission. Even more specific questions must also be answered in any attempt to arrive at fully justifiable cost figures for ALPAT. For example, a mix of several different types of equipment is employed in the conduct of ALPAT so we really need information on operating costs for types of units rather than a standardized figure for cutter days or aircraft hours. There are complex questions concerning the proper allocation of personnel benefits and retirement programs in attempting to separate the costs of fisheries law enforcement from the costs attributable to the Coast Guard's other missions. And there is no simple way to decide on appropriate amortization schedules for vessels and aircraft in efforts to compute the fixed costs of Coast Guard operations on an annual basis.

All this means that it would be hazardous to set too much store by any specific cost figures attached to the operation of ALPAT. Even so, it is of some interest to compute a rough-and-ready figure for the cost of this operation, and I have attempted to do so. In essence, I have accepted the Coast Guard's own figure for the nationwide cost of the program entitled enforcement of laws and treaties (ELT) and made suitable adjustments not only to distinguish between the enforcement of fisheries regulations and other regulations

or treaty requirements but also to separate the costs attributable to the North Pacific region from those incurred in other
regions.[27] The upshot of all this is an estimate of $18.5 mil-
lion for the total costs of ALPAT during fiscal year 1978.
While I would not wish to defend this figure very vigorously,
I suspect it is of the right order of magnitude for this
operation.

Recall, however, that the Coast Guard does not bear all
the costs of enforcing fisheries regulations in the North
Pacific. Thus, there is a fisheries management and enforcement operation carried out by NMFS, and all the relevant
legal work for fisheries enforcement is done by the General
Counsel's office of NOAA or the U.S. Attorney's office in
Anchorage. The costs of enforcing fisheries regulations in the
North Pacific borne by NMFS can be divided between the
Alaska Regional Office and headquarters in Washington. For
the Alaska Regional Office the relevant calculations are straightforward: enforcement activities accounted for 26.8 percent of
the budget or $745,500 during fiscal year 1978.[28] No com-
parable figures are available for the costs of headquarters
operations attributable to North Pacific enforcement, but the
total must be substantially smaller. As far as the legal work is
concerned, it is possible to raise various questions concerning
"billing" procedures and the extent to which court costs
should be attributed to the account of fisheries law enforcement. These costs can be safely assumed to be comparatively
small, however, since they consist primarily of personnel costs
in contrast to the costs of acquiring and operating expensive
equipment. Overall, it is probably not too wide of the mark
to conclude that the cost of the current FCMA enforcement
program for the North Pacific region is of the order of $20
million a year.

One factor still remains to be taken into account in
thinking about the costs of this enforcement program. There
can be no doubt that all enforcement activities generate
certain intangible costs, and the program under review here is

certainly no exception. In the case of FCMA enforcement, it is possible to separate these intangible costs into two categories: internal or domestic costs and international costs. The internal costs of ALPAT involve such things as the growth of bureaucratic rigidity associated with complex administrative procedures, the prospect of corruption (broadly defined) in conjunction with enforcement practices, and the alienation commonly experienced by subjects who are the targets of a somewhat heavy-handed enforcement system.[29] On the international side, there are costs attributable to overt unilateralism in an interdependent world. In such an environment, national enforcement can easily contribute to the growth of costly forms of neomercantilism and the decline of prospects for resolving international problems in a cooperative fashion. These international costs are particularly important in the North Pacific since the FCMA enforcement program in the region has been directed, at least so far, primarily toward foreign fishing vessels. Of course, it is impossible to quantify these intangible costs in any straightforward fashion. Therefore, it is understandable that they tend to be dropped from serious consideration in efforts to think about the efficiency of enforcement programs from a utilitarian perspective. Nonetheless, I would argue that this is a serious mistake in the case at hand. In the final analysis, it may well turn out that the intangible costs of fisheries enforcement in the North Pacific are substantial and difficult to reverse, even though they cannot be expressed in monetary terms.

Bearing in mind these problems concerning cost calculations, let us take a look at the benefits flowing from efforts to enforce fisheries regulations in the North Pacific. As might be expected, the problems here are considerably less tractable than those encountered in computing the costs of enforcement activities.[30] Ultimately, these benefit calculations should measure the value of the damage to the relevant fisheries or fish stocks which is avoided as a consequence of deterring or apprehending violations. This is so because the underlying purpose of the FCMA regulations is, or should be, to maintain the fisheries in a healthy condition so they can sustain commercial harvesting on a continuous basis. The basic rationale for the enforcement program rests on the contribution it can make to the achievement of this goal. Such a direct approach to the calculation of benefits, however, is fraught with problems already identified in the discussion of effectiveness. Human predation is only one factor affecting the condition of stocks of marine fish. Other factors, such as the condition of marine mammal stocks, trends in marine pollution, and the emergence of conflicting uses of the relevant marine areas, are apt to have as much impact on fish stocks as human predation. This is especially true of complex ecosystems involving multiple species, a condition that prevails in the North Pacific. Beyond this, with a few exceptions knowledge of the basic condition of the stocks and of population dynamics is not sufficient to permit direct calculations of the benefits of enforcement activities in the North Pacific. Therefore, quite apart from complications concerning such matters as establishing an appropriate metric and specifying a suitable discount rate, the basic information needed to compute the benefits of enforcement on a direct basis is lacking.

This difficulty suggests a search for surrogate measures of the benefits flowing from enforcement, and this is the path that most analysts have followed.[31] The first thing to notice about this approach is that several differentiable surrogates have been proposed; they differ radically from each other in their analytic content, and there are substantial discrepancies among the results they yield. Among these indirect measures of benefits, the following deserve note: (i) the value of the penalties paid by violators, (ii) the cost of deterring and apprehending violations, (iii) the value of the catch taken as a result of violations, and (iv) the value of the illegal catch that would be taken in the absence of the enforcement program. Several of these surrogates have practically nothing to recom-

mend them other than ease of quantification and they can be
dismissed with little discussion. Thus there is no clear-cut
formula for calculating penalties in connection with FCMA
violations, and the idea that penalties paid somehow approxi-
mate benefits flowing from enforcement is almost totally
arbitrary. The equation of benefits with the costs of producing public sector goods or services is a common enough practice, but it is typically more nearly an admission of ignorance
than a meaningful way to come to terms with the measurement of benefits in nonmarket settings.[32] Moreover, this
practice has obvious drawbacks when it comes to the assessment of efficiency either in marginal terms or in benefit/cost
terms.

The problems with the other proposed surrogates are
somewhat less obvious but nonetheless fundamental. Not
only is the value of the catch taken in conjunction with
detected and apprehended violations difficult to determine,
it is also unclear why this value should be thought of as a
measure of the benefits of enforcement. What proportion of
the catch found aboard violating vessels should be treated as
stemming from the relevant violations? In what market
should the catch be sold to determine its actual market
value?[33] Can we reach any systematic conclusions about the
relationship between the quantity of illegal fish taken by
known violators and the condition of the fisheries in question? By contrast, efforts to determine the value of the illegal
catch that would be taken in the absence of an enforcement
program raise all the problems outlined in our earlier discussion of the direct approach to measuring effectiveness. It
would require information concerning the variables labeled x
and y in that discussion. This is so because such an approach
to the benefits of enforcement rests on a measure of the
difference between the level of illegal fishing expected in the
absence of enforcement and the amount of illegal fishing that
will continue to occur even in the presence of the enforcement program. Consequently, this surrogate can hardly be

relied upon as a practical procedure for computing the benefits of enforcement under real-world conditions.

To make matters worse, all these surrogates rely upon
certain assumptions about violations of fisheries regulations
which are questionable at best. In each case, there is a need to
arrive at some specific figure concerning the number of violations suppressed by the enforcement program. Sometimes
this is necessitated by the nature of the surrogate employed,
and it is always required to make use of benefit figures in
reaching conclusions about efficiency. Note, however, that
this too assumes some solution to the problems of measuring
effectiveness outlined above. Next, each of these approaches
to the benefits of enforcement rests on an assumption to the
effect that it is reasonable to regard all violations as equal in
this context. In some cases, this is accomplished by omitting
certain violations from the calculus (for example, those not
resulting in monetary penalties or in the seizure of illegal
fish), while in other cases it merely means lumping all violations into a single category without reference to type. But the
discussion of effectiveness in the preceding section should be
sufficient to suggest the implausibility of all such assumptions. What sense does it make to equate the benefits flowing
from the suppression of procedural violations or even violations of gear restrictions with the benefits accruing from the
elimination of illegal practices relating to the retention of
prohibited species? Additionally, all of the surrogate approaches emphasize efforts to compute average values for
violations suppressed rather than the marginal benefits of
enforcement activities. Thus, the benefits of suppressing an
individual violation are treated equally whether it is the first
violation suppressed or the last. But this is obviously a
dubious practice. A small illegal catch may have little or no
impact on the condition of fish stocks, whereas extensive
violations may raise serious questions about the commercial
viability of the stocks in question. It follows that there will
ordinarily be declining marginal returns associated with the

enforcement of fisheries regulations and that those responsible for enforcement should be far more concerned about suppressing the first violations of a regulation than the last ones.

Assume now that we have wrestled with these problems of computing costs and benefits and arrived at some specific cost and benefit figures for the FCMA enforcement program in the North Pacific. How do we decide whether the existing program is efficient? There are at least three distinct tacks that can be taken in answering this question.[34] The tack suggested by neoclassical microeconomics emphasizes marginal analysis: enforcement activities in the North Pacific should be expanded until the marginal benefit flowing from the last unit of enforcement effort just equals the marginal cost of that unit.[35] To follow this tack we would need to construct marginal benefit and cost curves for enforcement of the type illustrated in figure 6. A moment's reflection, however, should make it clear that there is no hope of using this approach in any systematic empirical sense in the case of fisheries law enforcement. It is evident from the preceding discussion that it is difficult to arrive at figures for a single point on these curves, much less to plot the trajectory of the curves over any significant distance. Not only is it hard to come to terms with the costs and benefits of the existing enforcement program, it is also painfully clear that we can say little about the costs and benefits of alternative enforcement programs in the absence of empirical experience. Nevertheless, there is one important lesson to be drawn from this line of reasoning. Though it is impossible to specify the exact shapes of the marginal cost and benefit curves of figure 6, it is almost certainly reasonable to assume that increasing marginal costs and declining marginal benefits will set in at some stage in the realm of fisheries law enforcement. What this means is that, under any of a wide range of specific assumptions about the shapes of these curves, it will not be rational for the public authority sponsoring the enforcement program

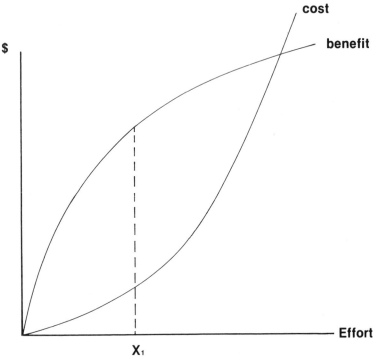

Fig. 6. Benefits and costs of enforcement as a function of effort. X_1 is level of effort at equilibrium, given the shape of the benefit and cost curves.

to make any effort to eliminate all violations of fisheries regulations or even to bring the level of violations close to zero.[36]

   A second tack concerning the question of efficiency involves the use of benefit/cost analysis.[37] The basic idea here is to compute a benefit/cost ratio for the enforcement program, ascertain whether the value of the ratio exceeds unity under reasonable assumptions, and compare this ratio to those that would emerge in connection with alternative programs. The first thing to notice about this approach is that it differs substantially from the marginal procedure outlined above. The two approaches are not logically equivalent; a policy alternative yielding the highest benefit/cost ratio need not be the alternative leading to optimal results in terms of marginal analysis.[38] And the benefit/cost approach does not facilitate continuous comparisons that would make it easy to judge the relative merits of alternative enforcement programs. At the same time, there are somewhat better reasons to hope that the benefit/cost approach can be used in a systematic, empirical fashion in evaluating efforts to enforce fisheries regulations. Even so, the practical problems are severe. It is difficult to arrive at justifiable figures for the costs and especially the benefits of the enforcement program in the North Pacific. What I have labeled intangible costs are generally simply ignored, and any estimates of benefits are bound to be crude and disputable at best.[39] The usual response to these problems is to offer several cost and benefit figures based on different assumptions and then to ask whether the resultant benefit/cost ratios are favorable across a range of these assumptions.[40] Though this is undoubtedly a useful step to take, it must be obvious at this point that there is great scope for manipulation in making these benefit/cost calculations and that it is apt to be relatively easy for those wishing to reach predetermined conclusions to adjust their computations of costs or benefits in such a way as to arrive at the desired results. Beyond this, benefit/cost analysis leaves much to be desired in any effort to compare the efficiency of the existing enforcement program in the North Pacific with fundamentally different approaches to the enforcement problem in this area (for example, the 100 percent observer proposal). It is one thing to make assumptions about the impact on costs or benefits of adding a few cutter days or aircraft hours to the current enforcement effort. It is far more difficult to assess the probable costs and benefits of fundamentally different approaches that have never been tried. In this sense, it is probably fair to say that benefit/cost analysis has a conservative bias, discouraging favorable consideration of qualitatively different policy options.

Yet a third tack that can be taken in considering the

efficiency of enforcement efforts goes under the heading of
cost-effectiveness analysis. The basic idea here is to decide at
the outset on the level of compliance with FCMA regulations
we wish to obtain and then to examine alternative enforcement procedures with an eye toward minimizing "the value
of resources used to attain the stated objective."[41] This
implies a recognition of the extreme problems afflicting
attempts to compute benefits with any precision coupled with
a determination to pursue a reasonable level of compliance
with fisheries regulations as a matter of general policy. By way
of comparison, this is the approach generally employed in the
realm of defense policy and often recommended by economists favoring the use of effluent charges as a method of
pursuing pollution control.[42] It might be a little awkward in
connection with the enforcement of fisheries regulations to
admit at the outset that perfect compliance is not even a
serious goal. But those who think about such problems carefully would hardly find this surprising, and it would not be
necessary to publicize this fact widely in any case. On the
positive side, this type of analysis tends to encourage systematic comparisons of the costs associated with alternative
policy instruments that can be used to attain the goal specified at the outset. For example, this is the analytic setting in
which the debate over the relative merits of charges and
regulations in the field of pollution control has unfolded in
recent years.[43] With respect to the enforcement of fisheries
regulations in the North Pacific, this approach would suggest
questions about the relative costs of relying on Coast Guard
operations, initiating a 100 percent observer program, taking
steps to structure the incentives of foreign governments in
appropriate ways, and making use of some mix of these
options. Of course, this approach to assessing the efficiency of
enforcement operations is hardly a panacea. Not only does it
leave the specification of the overall goal to ill-defined political processes, it also offers no magic formulas for computing
the expected costs of alternative enforcement programs that
have not yet been tried. In comparison with the tacks dis-

cussed above, however, this approach accommodates the available data in a considerably more realistic fashion.

What conclusions should be drawn from this discussion of the issue of efficiency in conjunction with efforts to enforce fisheries regulations in the North Pacific? Above all, it suggests that there are serious questions about the usefulness of utilitarian thinking in situations of this type.[44] To put it mildly, the results obtained through the use of these procedures are apt to be crude and disputable. Therefore, it is always important in discussions of this sort to resist the temptation to equate the use of numbers with the achievement of analytic precision. Additionally, it is well to remember that efficiency calculations in such nonmarket settings are typically manipulable to such an extent that they can be used to rationalize any of a wide range of predetermined policy prescriptions. The results obtained from such calculations are entirely dependent on the assumptions underlying them, and it should be apparent that there is ample scope for debate concerning appropriate assumptions to be used in computing the costs and benefits associated with efforts to enforce fisheries regulations. It follows that there is some danger that the use of these procedures will do more harm than good in conjunction with specific policy problems, unless participants in the debate can be relied upon to adhere to reasonable standards of integrity in using such procedures. Beyond this, it would be a mistake to assume that efficiency calculations of this type play a large role in actual policymaking, even when policy debates are superficially clothed in the language of benefit/cost or cost-effectiveness analysis. Major decisions concerning the enforcement program for fisheries regulations have an ineradicable political element that is hardly likely to vanish just because some of the relevant arguments are deployed in the language of efficiency calculations. If used with restraint, however, it seems to me that analytic procedures aimed at assessing the efficiency of enforcement programs have an important contribution to make. Not only do they raise questions about saving resources in the operation of existing enforcement programs, they also force one to think about radically different approaches to the enforcement problem as well as the basic goals that should be pursued in the realm of fisheries law enforcement.

This brings us to another implication of this discussion of efficiency. Are there fundamental alternatives to the present method of obtaining compliance with FCMA regulations in the North Pacific? Assuming that we retain the basic character of the FCMA regime, it strikes me that there are two major alternatives to the current enforcement program that features the operation of ALPAT by the Coast Guard. At least for foreign fishing vessels, we might attempt to get the relevant foreign governments to play a greater role in enforcing FCMA regulations on their own nationals. This would involve either taking steps to alter the incentive structures facing these governments or shifting the formal burden of proof concerning compliance to them through some device such as threatening to withhold the issuance of fishing permits. Alternatively, we could implement the 100 percent observer proposal. The essence of this proposal is to place full-time observers on all foreign vessels operating within the FCZ and to charge these observers with enforcement duties as well as responsibility for gathering data.[45] Each of these ideas deserves further consideration, but I think it is important to proceed with other parts of this study before attempting to come to terms with these alternatives. Therefore, I return to these proposals in the final substantive section of this chapter, where it is possible to examine them in the light of my completed assessment of the current FCMA enforcement program in the North Pacific.

If we drop the assumption that the FCMA regime retains its basic character, it is possible to identify more drastic changes in the entire regime which would have far-reaching implications for the problem of enforcement. Thus, we might consider shifting from a system emphasizing administrative regulations to one relying much more heavily on economic incentives. The issues here are quite similar to those involved in the regulations/charges debate in the field of pollution control.[46] The basic idea would be to charge fishermen for engaging in various activities in the fisheries rather than to proscribe these activities and to mete out penalties for violations of the relevant proscriptions. Going a step further, we might simply divide the marine fisheries into specified marine sanctuaries where no fishing at all would be permitted and other areas where fishermen would be free to fish on a relatively unrestricted basis.[47] Under such a regime, enforcement would be largely irrelevant in the unrestricted areas, and it would take the form of supervising a general closure with respect to the sanctuaries. There can be no doubt that this type of enforcement would be substantially less expensive than the current program, and it would certainly appeal to those who feel that enforcing an extensive network of detailed regulations is a losing proposition in a region the size of the North Pacific. It strikes me that both of these alternatives deserve further study. But each of them would require major changes in the current FCMA regime. Under the circumstances, a careful study of these alternatives would carry us well beyond the scope of this chapter, and I shall therefore set them aside for investigation on another occasion.

EQUITY

Do those who benefit from the operation of the FCMA enforcement program generally shoulder the costs attributable to the program or is this an activity resulting in significant in-kind transfers? More specifically, who pays for the enforcement of fisheries regulations in the North Pacific? Who benefits from the enforcement of these regulations? What is the relationship between those who pay for enforcement and the beneficiaries? Is this relationship easy to justify on normative grounds or does it give rise to serious questions concerning equity?

In the first instance, the costs of enforcing FCMA regulations in the North Pacific are borne by the U.S. federal government. Though they may not be itemized in a manner that is easy to comprehend, these costs are reflected in the annual budgets of the Coast Guard, the National Marine Fisheries Service, and the Department of Justice. As I indicated above, all these costs taken together probably run about $20 million a year under current conditions. Perhaps the first thing to notice about these costs is that they are not offset by the receipt of economic returns from the fisheries on the part of the federal government. In this respect, the situation differs from that prevailing in connection with other natural resources under federal control. Thus, existing regimes call for the public sector to receive economic returns from outer continental shelf oil and gas and from timber harvested on federally owned land, though the extent to which these returns are adequate is a highly controversial matter.[48] Whatever the reasoning behind this situation, therefore, the government cannot charge off enforcement costs against returns accruing to it as the owner or manager of the pertinent stocks of fish.[49]

In contrast, some of the costs of enforcement are offset by fees, penalties, and observer costs paid by foreign fishermen. Thus, section 204(b)(10) of the FCMA specifies that "Reasonable fees shall be paid to the Secretary by the owner or operator of any foreign fishing vessel for which a permit is issued pursuant to this subsection," and the language of the section makes it clear that enforcement costs can be taken into account in setting these fees. Currently, these section 204 fees are set at one dollar per gross registered ton and 3.5 percent of the ex-vessel value of the catch.[50] As I indicated above, penalties are authorized under the terms of sections 308 to 310 of the FCMA.[51] Note also in this connection that in cases involving gross violations, fishing vessels or their catch may be subject to civil forfeiture, and proceeds from the sale of these items might well go to offset general enforcement costs should they exceed expenses directly attributable to the forfeiture proceedings. Finally, section 201(C)(2)(d) requires that "duly authorized United States observers be permitted on board any [foreign fishing] vessel and that the United States be reimbursed for the cost of such observers." Under present circumstances, this provision merely serves to negate the cost to the U.S. federal government of mounting a modest observer program primarily for the purpose of collecting data needed in making management decisions. It is obvious, however, that the provision would become far more important in conjunction with any move to adopt the 100 percent observer proposal.

Table 9 gives some indication of the magnitude of these fees, penalties, and observer costs for the North Pacific region during the period since the implementation of the FCMA on 1 March 1977. Note that revenues from fees and penalties do not begin to match the roughly $20 million a year which it costs to enforce FCMA regulations in the North Pacific. At the same time, there is no indication that fees and penalties are currently set with an eye toward offsetting the costs of enforcing fisheries regulations. In fact, it is evident that there is no clear-cut rationale underlying the existing structure of fees and penalties, though this is an area where significant changes may occur during the foreseeable future.[52] Additionally, the size of penalties (but not fees) is subject to vigorous bargaining on a case-by-case basis between attorneys for the federal government and attorneys for the fishermen. Finally, it is important to bear in mind that none of these revenues can be used directly to offset the costs of enforcing FCMA regulations. All such revenues go initially into the U.S. Treasury, and the money required to pay the expenses of the enforcement program must be appropriated by Congress. While this may at first seem like an accounting detail, it is actually a fact of considerable political importance.[53] It means that the Coast Guard and NMFS cannot use revenue generated by the enforcement program to cover their expenses and that these agencies must regularly satisfy congressional committees in order to carry on the FCMA enforcement program.

The preceding discussion focuses on the direct or first-order incidence of the costs of enforcing FCMA regulations in

TABLE 9
FCMA REVENUES
NORTH PACIFIC REGION—1978

	Japan	USSR	Korea	Other	Total
Fees[a]	$6,039,241	$2,128,674	$412,525	$24,644	$8,605,084
Penalties[b]	218,270	23,000	0	0	241,270
Observer costs[c]	759,984	113,796	41,321	0	915,101

[a]FCMA fees currently include $1 per gross registered ton plus 3.5% of the ex-vessel value of the catch. While the gross registered ton fees are not computed on a regional basis, I have adjusted them to encompass only the North Pacific region and combined these adjusted fees with poundage fees for the region.

[b]These figures include penalties for violations occurring in 1978 paid as of 18 October 1979. Since some 1978 violations remained unsettled as of that date, total penalties paid for 1978 violations will eventually be somewhat higher.

[c]Observer costs are billed directly to each foreign nation by NMFS. To date, these costs have been paid by making suitable deductions from refunds on poundage fees originally paid.

SOURCES: Permits and Regulations Division, NMFS and Law Enforcement Division, NMFS.

the North Pacific. But who ultimately pays for this enforcement program? The answer to this question comes in two distinct parts. The fees, penalties, and observer costs are reflected in increased costs of production for the fishing industry. They simply become a part of the costs of doing business, and they will be treated like any other cost of production. Such costs can either be passed along to consumers or they can be absorbed by the fishing companies. In the case at hand, it seems safe to assume that these added costs will be largely passed on to consumers. Even in Japan, the fishing industry typically operates with a relatively small profit margin. Soviet commissars as well as Japanese capitalists have strong incentives to keep their rate of return or profit margin as high as possible. And the fishing industry as a whole is not characterized by the type of competition that would make it impossible to pass along the costs of fees and penalties to consumers. Notice in this connection that the consumer groups affected by the resultant increases in market prices are sometimes Americans. While the Soviet Union does not export any amount of fish or fish products to the United States, Japan has exported a large and growing proportion of its commercial harvests to the United States. In 1978, for example, the United States imported $256,827,000 worth of fish and fish products from Japan, which amounted to 8.3 percent of American imports of these products from the world as a whole.

As the figures presented in table 9 suggest, however, all these fees, penalties, and so forth currently account for a relatively small proportion of the cost of enforcing FCMA regulations in the North Pacific. The bulk of the costs are consequently borne by the federal government, which means that they are ultimately shouldered by the American taxpaying public. Since the current tax structure at the federal level is somewhat progressive, those members of the taxpaying public with intermediate incomes are paying for a proportionately greater share of the enforcement program than those with lower incomes. But there is no reason to believe that the resultant incidence of the costs of enforcement correlates highly with the pattern of consumption of fish and fish products in the United States. On the contrary, with the exception of certain highly valued species (for example, shrimp and some crabs), there is good reason to conclude that the quantity of fish consumed by the American public is inversely correlated with income. Under the circumstances, if the enforcement program contributes to the maintenance of healthy fish stocks so that supplies remain plentiful and prices do not rise rapidly, the result can be conceptualized as an in-kind transfer from the wealthier strata to the poorer strata of society. Should the net result be merely to drive up the cost of fish to the consumer, however, this would amount to a program under which the wealthier members of society pay for activities which make life more costly for the poorer members. Of course, such a program can be justified in terms of protecting natural environments, but it should hardly be surprising if it were not greeted with enthusiasm by members of the lower socioeconomic strata of the society.

All this leads me directly to several questions concerning equity. To begin with, why should the public subsidize fishermen by footing the bill for the FCMA enforcement program? It is bad enough that the public sector receives no economic return on this natural resource, though this may be explained away in terms of the generally unprofitable condition of the fishing industry during recent times. But is there any reason why the public should pay the cost of extricating the fishermen from the problems associated with an unrestricted common property regime? Why not let the fishermen themselves band together to solve these problems, perhaps even hiring the government to provide enforcement for the rules they adopt? As far as I can see, the principal justification for the current arrangement under which the public pays for much of the enforcement program stems from the notion that there is a collective goods aspect to fisheries management. By

maintain the viability of natural environments. But this hardly eliminates the normative problem raised by such an arrangement. What can be done about this situation? Once again, I would argue that some sort of fee system constitutes a preferred alternative. While we must assume that producers will pass through a large proportion of these fees to consumers of fish and fish products, this is not necessarily bad. Consumers would be paying the costs of operating a restricted common property system in the fisheries, and these costs seem to me to be legitimate costs of production.[60] The result would be a growing assurance of healthy fish stocks in the future that would sustain the supply of fish and fish products. In fact, it is possible that such a system could be used to achieve limited entry, thereby increasing the efficiency of the fishing industry so that costs of production and perhaps prices to the consumer would go down.[61] In any case, consumers would end up paying prices determined by the costs of production for fish and fish products rather than helping to underwrite the goals of those concerned with the protection of natural environments. Yet the natural environments in question, the fish stocks and the fishing grounds, would be retained in good condition as a by-product of the regime I have advocated.

THE CONDUCT OF ENFORCEMENT

So far, I have examined the enforcement of fisheries regulations in aggregate terms, raising questions about the effectiveness, efficiency, and equity of the FCMA enforcement program taken as a whole. Now it is time to disaggregate these issues and to consider the conduct of enforcement operations on a day-to-day basis. This requires an analysis of the attitudes, behavior, and enforcement practices of those who carry out these operations from the level of individual boarding officers to the level of attorneys handling the disposition of cases arising in connection with specific enforcement incidents.

In the course of this enquiry I hope to shed some light

on several major controversies concerning regulation in general. Recent theoretical work on regulation emphasizes the extent to which "economic regulation serves the private interests of politically effective groups."[62] In many cases, these are groups associated with the regulated industry itself, but effective pressures are also brought to bear by other interests (for example, environmental groups) in some regulatory situations. Supplementing these pressures are the impacts of bureaucratic goals pursued by regulatory agencies as well as the personal concerns of individual regulators. The upshot is a regulatory system responsive to the interplay of political demand and supply in contrast to the pursuit of the public interest.[63]

Most often, these arguments are articulated in conjunction with analyses of the choice of basic regulatory policies and the promulgation of specific regulations. But the basic line of reasoning is clearly applicable to the problem of obtaining compliance with regulations as well. As Freeman and Haveman put it,

Regulatory agencies have substantial discretionary power concerning the interpretation and application of their rule-making and enforcement powers. As a consequence, regulation/enforcement becomes essentially a political process entailing bargaining between parties of unequal power. In this process the real issues are camouflaged in technical jargon, and the regulators are largely isolated from political accountability for their actions. The regulatory agency and the interests they regulate bargain over the regulations to be set. They bargain over whether violations have occurred and, if so, who was responsible. They bargain over what steps shall be taken to correct infractions. . . . At every stage of this multi-level bargaining process those being regulated have a lot at stake, while the public interest is diffuse, poorly organized, and poorly represented. Predictably, the bargains struck favor those being regulated.[64]

To what extent does this constitute an accurate portrayal of experience to date with the FCMA enforcement program? Does this experience depart significantly from the expectations generated by recent theoretical work, and if so, how can we account for such departures? The discussion that follows constitutes an attempt to formulate answers to these questions on the basis of an in-depth investigation of the North Pacific region.

Some general observations about enforcing fisheries regulations in the North Pacific are in order at the outset. The situation at hand does not conform to the classic image of what enforcement is all about.[65] Specifically, it is not characterized by the presence of a set of simple rules, the existence of well-defined "beats" for enforcement officers, and the prospect of straightforward, yes-or-no decisions regarding most infractions. The fundamental objectives underlying FCMA regulations do not require the achievement of perfect compliance. It is sufficient to deter or apprehend major violations to keep the fish stocks generally healthy. The complexity of the regulations combined with the nature of high seas fishing operations frequently makes it diffficult to reach conclusions about possible infractions on any cut-and-dried basis. And the size of the region is such that it would be prohibitively expensive to blanket the area with enforcement patrols on a continuous basis. Under the circumstances, it makes sense to approach the problem of enforcing FCMA regulations in the North Pacific from a managerial point of view. It is more important to curb grossly inappropriate practices on the part of the industry as a whole than to worry about the details of specific infractions involving individual fishing vessels. This suggests, in turn, that the occurrence of much bargaining is neither surprising nor inappropriate in this domain. Any attempt to pursue all potential violators in a classic enforcement mode would quickly become excessively cumbersome.

It is also important to realize that there is great latitude for discretion or the exercise of judgment in connection with the FCMA enforcement program[66] at all levels of the operation. Individual boarding officers have considerable leeway concerning the things they look for, the search procedures they favor, and the intensity with which they carry out boardings. Commanding officers of Coast Guard vessels can and do exercise judgment continuously concerning such matters as courses to follow on ALPAT patrols, the selection of specific vessels to board, and the handling of individual cases as they arise on the high seas. Officials in Juneau (both Coast Guard and NMFS) have a lot of freedom in formulating instructions for individual patrols as well as in dealing with specific enforcement incidents once contact is made in the field with an alleged violator. And it is clear that there is ample scope for discretion in the disposition of cases, whether they are handled administratively through NOAA or more formally through the U.S. Attorney's office in Anchorage.

The major factors contributing to this situation are not hard to identify. There is considerable ambiguity in the language of many individual regulations, and it is difficult to devise objective measures of the effectiveness of various enforcement practices that might be emphasized in an effort to standardize ALPAT activities. The logistical problems involved in carrying out an enforcement operation over an area the size of the North Pacific make it necessary to cope with many situations on an ad hoc or nonstandardized basis. The command structure of the Coast Guard, essentially a military organization, places extensive discretion in the hands of certain officers whether they like it or not. Perhaps the most striking case in point is the commanding officer of a vessel, an individual whose word is law while the vessel is under way on any given mission. And the administrative arrangements associated with the enforcement of fisheries regulations offer few opportunities to overcome the effects of variability in judgment calls during prior phases of the operation. Not only are these arrangements highly sensitive to political pressure themselves, it also takes a long time to accumulate a stream of authoritative legal interpretations relating to ambiguous aspects of the FCMA enforcement program. To illustrate, the federal courts have yet to provide any clear-cut guidance with respect to numerous controversial practices employed in the North Pacific enforcement operation (for example, the absence of search warrants and preliminary hearings in conjunction with seizures). That this situation is easy to explain, however, should not be allowed to obscure its consequences. It is clear that there is substantial variation in the treatment of individual cases involving actual or potential violations of FCMA regulations in the North Pacific. This applies to judgments concerning the seriousness of violations (that is, the extent to which any given situation warrants a citation, a violation, or a seizure) as well as the occurrence of impermissible activities in the first instance. In my judgment, these discretionary variations in the North Pacific do not exhibit any systematic bias. Thus, I have observed no evidence of a pattern of anti-Japanese or anti-Soviet enforcement actions or of a trend suggesting discrimination against medium stern trawlers or crab factories. Nonetheless, the absence of systematic bias hardly constitutes a basis for concluding that the consequences of this situation are trivial. There is little doubt that we are departing significantly from the ideal of equal justice in our efforts to enforce FCMA regulations in the North Pacific. That departures from this ideal probably occur on a more or less random basis is certainly cold comfort for those who have been or may become victims of such practices.

Moreover, the existence of great latitude for the exercise of judgment makes the FCMA enforcement program vulnerable to the impact of fashions and fads relating to specific enforcement practices. In some cases, altering practices constitutes a reasonable response to prior experience and deserves to be applauded. When extensive discretion is coupled with a lack of objective measures of effectiveness, however, such changes are apt to spring from a desire to promote some "new look" or to convey an impression of innovativeness. While this is not an easy matter on which to pass judgment, I am persuaded that fashion has played a substantial role in promoting changes in the enforcement practices employed in the North Pacific during the period since 1 March 1977. Turn now to some more specific issues pertaining to the conduct of enforcement operations in the North Pacific.

Guiding Images

There are great differences of outlook among those participating in the North Pacific enforcement program with respect to the fundamental nature of the problem. At one extreme, some participants assume that all fishermen are violators; the basic problem is to devise methods of apprehending them with limited enforcement capabilities. Others believe that it is only necessary to maintain an enforcement presence. That is, while fishermen may well develop impermissible habits if no attempt at surveillance is made, few of them are likely to undertake any conscious or sustained attempt to engage in violations in the face of even a modest enforcement program. Still others argue that the most important concern is for the enforcers to avoid becoming an undue nuisance to law-abiding fishermen. They assume that fishermen should be free to carry on normal operations without harassment on the part of those assigned to enforce regulations. And of course there are numerous variations on these outlooks which ensure the existence of a wide spectrum of guiding images relating to the enforcement of fisheries regulations in the North Pacific.

There is no obvious method of determining which of these guiding images is correct. This follows from the same problems that obstruct efforts to arrive at objective conclusions concerning the effectiveness of programs designed to enforce fisheries regulations. Nonetheless, some comments about the behavior of fishermen are in order at this juncture. Perhaps the most influential earlier study of this problem proceeds from the "fundamental behavioral assumption . . . that fishermen, in general, do not intentionally set out to violate a given statute or agreement; their primary motivation is to catch as many fish as possible.''[67] This assumption seems unexceptionable as far as it goes. It is hard to see any basis for concluding that fishermen would violate FCMA regulations as an end in itself. But this does not take us much beyond rather arbitrary statements to the effect that ''In the absence of any enforcement efforts, there exists a steady-state probability of violation.''[68]

Under the circumstances, it seems important to revert to several observations set forth in the introduction to this chapter. Even under the FCMA, the regime for marine fisheries is essentially a common property system, and the perverse incentives intrinsic to common property remain operative. Further, the financial stakes involved in the North Pacific fisheries are substantial. Therefore, we must assume that fishermen will in fact violate regulations designed to conserve fish stocks on a regular basis in the absence of a serious enforcement program. It does not require a bleak view of human nature to reach this conclusion; it follows from the operation of self-interest in conjunction with a problematic structure of rights and rules. Of course, it is possible that there are substantial variations among groups of fishermen in this regard. For example, Japanese fishermen, as members of a compliance culture, may be more likely than Russian fishermen to adhere to fisheries regulations in the absence of an enforcement program. This is obviously a complex topic, involving subtle patterns of behavior that are difficult to observe. Nevertheless, I have not yet encountered evidence of significant differences along these lines among fishermen in the North Pacific.

Enforcement Tactics

Given what I have said about discretion and guiding images, it should come as no surprise to learn that there are extensive differences of opinion among those involved in enforcing fisheries regulations concerning effective or appropriate tactics for accomplishing the enforcement mission. It

turns out that there are numerous tactical questions to consider in conjunction with ALPAT patrols. What is the best
course to plot on a given patrol? Which fishing vessels should
be selected for boarding during a particular period of time? Is
it desirable to "hit" recently boarded vessels again on the
grounds that the fishing masters of such vessels may expect to
be free from inspection for some time? How thoroughly
should a vessel be searched if a preliminary inspection fails to
turn up any sign of infractions? What factors (for example,
records keeping, the condition of holds, the treatment of
prohibited species) should be stressed during any given
boarding? When a cutter has a helicopter deployed, how can
it be used to best advantage in connection with the enforcement operation? Under what conditions does it make sense to
run "silent' (in contrast to running "noisy") in the hope of
catching potential violators by surprise? What are the
prospects of making use of islands for camouflage so that a
cutter can pounce on unsuspecting violators? Are there
opportunities to coordinate the movements of several cutters
to employ what is known as a stake-out in ordinary police
work?

In part, judgments concerning these matters stem from
the objective conditions prevailing in the North Pacific. To
illustrate, it is always justifiable to pay close attention to the
100-fathom curve in the central Bering Sea, and stake-outs
cannot be used extensively when a small number of cutters
must patrol an area the size of the North Pacific. Nonetheless, much of the variation in this realm is attributable to
differences in the guiding images and past experiences of the
officers involved in the program. My impression is that there
is some correlation between age or extent of experience in the
enforcement of fisheries regulations and a preference for
tactics designed to expose sophisticated violators. But I
cannot say whether this is a function of age per se, the particular era in which those now holding relatively senior positions came of age, or a tendency to become somewhat

jaundiced as a consequence of long involvement with enforcement.

Diligence

There is no indication that those responsible for enforcing FCMA regulations in the North Pacific have been coopted by the subjects of these regulations.[69] I have observed occasional friendly gestures between the two sides in this arena (for example, the exchange of small gifts). But it is clear that the enforcers do not collude with the fishermen, bending the regulations in exchange for payoffs or kickbacks of any kind. Of course, this enforcement operation is directed largely toward foreign fishermen. Accordingly, some may question whether the same level of diligence is likely to occur when the operation is extended to cover domestic fishermen on a regular basis. In my judgment, the answer to this question is yes. As I have indicated, ALPAT is carried out primarily by the Coast Guard, an organization with a distinct military tradition and outlook. With respect to this issue, the military character of the Coast Guard is apt to serve us in good stead. Not only does the Coast Guard have no special relationship with the fishing industry, individual officers are also taught to be diligent in following both detailed instructions and the commands of superior officers.

Additionally, those participating in enforcement operations in the North Pacific clearly make a real effort to catch violators. There are indications that some participants lack a sophisticated understanding of the nature of the enforcement problem in this realm. I am convinced that there is some tendency to fix on surrogate indicators of performance (for example, the frequency of enforcement incidents), a practice that diverts attention from the real problems of enforcing fisheries regulations. And it is clear that there is some danger of cutters being diverted to other missions (for example, search and rescue) in a way that makes significant inroads on the effectiveness of enforcement operations in the fisheries.

In my judgment, this suggests a need to upgrade the enforcement mission in the future and to structure incentives in such a way as to motivate officers to acquire genuine sophistication in the realm of enforcing fisheries regulations. But none of this leads me to conclude that there is any lack of diligence on the part of FCMA enforcement personnel in the North Pacific.

Letter vs. Spirit

In a sense, the current enforcement operation exhibits a tendency toward overzealousness. Specifically, I have observed evidence of an excessively literal or picky application of regulations under real-world conditions. In part, this may reflect nothing more than what Wilson describes as the legalistic style of enforcement.[70] But it becomes a matter for serious consideration when it leads to an excessive flow of trivial citations or the issuance of violations for actions that cannot possibly have a significant impact on the health of the fish stocks. Even more serious, I have encountered some officers who become fired up by the idea of finding some grounds for issuing violations against specific fishing vessels. That is, they want to "throw the book" at alleged violators. Not only does this attitude reflect a lack of understanding of the managerial character of the enforcement problem in the North Pacific, it is also an outlook that would not be appropriate even in situations conforming more closely to the classic image of enforcement.

The sources of this overzealousness are relatively easy to pinpoint. Above all, they lie in the incentive structure associated with this enforcement operation. In the absence of any objective measures of effectiveness, there is an inevitable need to demonstrate performance or productivity, especially in some quantifiable form. While I have seen no evidence of the existence of any enforcement quotas for the North Pacific, there can be no doubt that feelings of concern about the performance of the enforcement program are widespread.

In addition, Coast Guard officers receive no systematic training in the realm of law enforcement. On the contrary, they are socialized to play by the book and to follow detailed instructions without undue questioning. Of course, experience with enforcement operations in the North Pacific might be expected to offset these deficiencies in training to a considerable degree. But this hope is largely undermined by the Coast Guard's policy of rotating officers rapidly from one assignment to another. Not only do officers tend to leave the region just when they are beginning to accumulate enough experience to be useful, they typically rotate out to a series of assignments that have nothing to do with enforcement at all. I view this combination of circumstances as a serious problem affecting the FCMA enforcement program, and I shall have more to say about it when I come to the formulation of recommendations.

Coordination

It should be obvious by now that the enforcement of fisheries regulations in the North Pacific requires extensive coordination.[71] There is a clear need to coordinate the efforts of the Coast Guard and NMFS, whether or not there is a NMFS agent present during any given enforcement incident. Equally interesting, there are complex coordination problems between individual units in the field and district headquarters in Juneau. These problems tend to arise in two distinct areas: the selection and location of individual vessels for boarding and the handling of ambiguous cases once contact has been made in the field. Not surprisingly, those on each side of this fence have their own perspective and complaints. On the one hand, officers in the field often feel that those operating at the district level fail to appreciate the difficulty of locating specific vessels in an area the size of the Bering Sea, do not always understand the need for speed in transmitting information, and have a hard time comprehending the nuances of complex cases as they unfold in the field.

Those in Juneau, on the other hand, are sensitive to political pressures emanating from Anchorage or Washington and feel that they are in a better position than those in the field to comprehend the big picture in any case. Additionally, this situation appears to be made somewhat more difficult by ambiguities concerning rank and the command structure. For example, the commanding officer of a cutter on an ALPAT mission is apt to outrank the head of the enforcement section at 17th District Headquarters, and yet the latter is commonly in the position of having to send formal instructions or orders to units in the field. I am persuaded on the basis of my own experiences that there is considerable room for improvement, at least in the North Pacific, with respect to these problems of coordination between units in the field and district head-quarters. From what I have already said, however, it should be clear that these problems are not fundamentally techno-logical in character. Rather, I believe they stem largely from matters of training, individual experience, and organizational routine which make it hard to put together a smoothly func-tioning and well-tested enforcement team for the region.

Disposition of Cases

Catching violators at sea hardly terminates the cycle of enforcement under the FCMA regime. Until recently, most of the work involved in disposing of North Pacific enforcement incidents was carried out by NMFS agents and NOAA attorneys, since there were only two seizures resulting from violations of FCMA regulations in the region prior to the beginning of 1979. At first, an effort was made to handle cases involving citations and violations on a relatively cen-tralized basis in Washington. It soon became clear, however, that this procedure was excessively cumbersome, and a decision was made in mid-1978 to decentralize these admini-strative processes to regional offices in an effort to speed up the disposition of cases. From all reports, this shift has produced a substantial improvement in the handling of

North Pacific cases. By contrast, the disposition of cases involving gross violations or seizures through the U.S. Attorney's office is a remarkably slow process. In part, this is undoubtedly attributable to lack of routine for such cases. But it is also a function of the protracted procedures involved in litigating significant cases in the federal courts. The major implication of this situation is that a large gap remains with regard to authoritative legal judgments concerning many of the most controversial aspects of the FCMA enforcement program.

I can see no grounds for concluding that the disposition of North Pacific enforcement incidents has been handled in such a way as to cater to the interests of private groups. But this is by no means equivalent to saying that the process of disposition is trouble free. There are unfortunate delays and, at least in connection with seizures, questionable practices that are costly to those being penalized for violations. The process begins to bog down when a large number of somewhat dubious citations and violations are passed along as a consequence of overzealousness on the part of units in the field. As with other regulatory arrangements, the disposition of cases tends to become an elaborate bargaining process. And the legitimacy of the results produced by this process is called into question because there exist no clear-cut or even consciously articulated formulas for the determination of penalties in specific cases. To make matters worse, I would expect this whole situation to become more problematic as we shift increasingly to cases involving domestic fishermen. On balance, these fishermen will be more knowledgeable and better situated to protect their interests through the American political and legal systems.

Civil Rights

It is obviously difficult to enforce a complex system of regulations in a region the size of the North Pacific. Under the circumstances, it is perhaps understandable that those responsible for enforcement would argue for the use of extraordinary measures and attempt to devise a structure of legal rights favoring those on the side of the enforcement program. This is exactly what has occurred in connection with the FCMA regime. The enforcers assert that it is permissible to search a fishing vessel without a warrant, seize a vessel without a preliminary hearing, refuse to release a seized vessel on bond, and revoke a fishing permit for an extended period of time without a preliminary hearing. The legal justification for the assertion of these powers rests on the proposition that fishing within the fishery conservation zone constitutes a "pervasively regulated" industry, not covered by the full range of constitutionaly protected civil rights. In practical terms, however, the justification for these extraordinary measures arises from the argument that they are necessary to assure the conservation of heavily used fish stocks.

There is no doubt that the difficulties of those attempting to enforce fisheries regulations in the North Pacific are real. But the curtailment of civil rights is a serious matter, and it seems reasonable to place a heavy burden of proof on those who would attempt to persuade us of the need for curtailment in specific cases. Ultimately, we must weigh the benefits of resource conservation against the benefits of upholding expansive views of civil rights, and there is every reason to expect that different commentators will disagree on such matters in specific cases. In my own judgment, the balance is now tipped dangerously in the direction of curtailment with respect to enforcement practices in the North Pacific. To illustrate, I find it hard to come up with a compelling justification for such practices as the issuance of violations on the basis of affidavits that are not corroborated by on-site inspections, the issuance of violations ex post facto after an initial failure to do so and the passage of considerable time, and the refusal to release a seized vessel on bond where it is evident that enforced idleness will prove extremely costly. In short, I think there is a need for a careful review of this set of issues now that the FCMA has been in operation long enough for some significant patterns to emerge.

Private Assistance

Those who are most criticial of the performance of regulators often argue that they are poorly informed about the behavior of those actually subject to the regulations. The thought here is that regulators are frequently among the last to find out what is going on in the real world, while various private citizens may acquire much information about such matters in the course of their day-to-day activities. It follows that those interested in enforcing regulations should rely much more heavily on private parties and reduce the scale of formal enforcement programs organized in the public sector.[72] This might well make it possible to cut costs substantially and to improve the quality of information about the behavior of subjects.

In fact, some effort has been made to pursue this idea in conjunction with the enforcement of FCMA regulations in the North Pacific. For example, the ALPAT manual encourages commanders of vessels on fisheries patrol in the area to put into various harbors in the hope of picking up useful information about actual or potential violations. Nonetheless, there are compelling reasons to conclude that this practice will not prove very helpful in the case at hand. To begin with, few private parties come into contact with the high seas fishing fleet during the course of fishing operations in the North Pacific. That is, the situation is hardly comparable to that arising in connection with regulations pertaining to work safety or even sport fishing. Equally important, those few private parties who might have useful information are apt to be poorly informed or to have axes of their own to grind. The FCMA regulations are complex, and there is ample evidence of widespread misconceptions concerning their content on the part of the general public. This is especially true with regard to restrictions on the activities of foreign fishermen. At the same time, those private interventions that do occur are apt to come from parties (or their representatives) charged with violations themselves who have obvious incentives to distort the truth in the interests of mitigating their own problems.[73] My impression is that the difficulties associated with information of this sort are just as severe in the case of fisheries regulations in the North Pacific as they are in any other realm involving powerful economic interests.

Oversight

Effective oversight is frequently proposed as a means of controlling undesirable or inappropriate practices in the field of regulation, but it is rarely used to good advantage.[74] What are the prospects for oversight in conjunction with the FCMA enforcement program? There are two fundamentally different streams of appraisal to be considered here: congressional oversight and independent auditing. Congressional oversight involves the organization of committee hearings or the conduct of systematic appraisals on the part of groups like the Office of Technology Assessment (OTA) and the General Accounting Office (GAO). Interestingly, each of these avenues has been pursued in the case of the FCMA enforcement program. The GAO has published a study of the problem, and congressional hearings have been held on the subject.[75] The overwhelming advantage of congressional oversight is the access to pertinent information that can be obtained by pursuing this tack. But this advantage is offset by several major drawbacks. Congressional hearings are political dramas rather than serious efforts to advance our understanding of public policy problems. And Congress lacks the expertise or the incentive to obtain the services of outside experts required to deal with oversight in any objective fashion. Groups like the GAO, in contrast, have neither the resources nor the analytic skills needed to come up with conclusions that carry us much beyond the level of common sense observations. For example, those who compiled the recent GAO study of enforcement never went to sea on an enforcement mission, which means that they did not have the benefit of experiencing the operation at first hand much less of participating in actual enforcement boardings. Therefore, while I certainly do not wish to suggest that congressional oversight is valueless, I regard it as a weak reed to lean on for those concerned about controlling enforcement operations carried out under the FCMA.

As things stand now, the notion of independent auditing refers to activities on the part of the media, public interest groups, and unattached scholars. Though I obviously would not want to write off appraisals emanating from these sources, I think it would be a mistake to expect very much from them. The overwhelming problem plaguing independent auditors involves access to pertinent information. The dawning of the era of freedom of information has done little to change this situation. As a practical matter, it is excruciatingly difficult for outside auditors to obtain anything like a full record of the activities of bureaucratic agencies. This is especially true in a situation like the one at hand where there are several agencies involved, each of which is jealous of its own prerogatives and highly sensitive to possible criticisms of its performance. Beyond this, independent auditors are apt to have axes of their own to grind or to lack the resources necessary to carry out full-blown assessments. Those responsible for enforcing FCMA regulations have become so sensitive to the presence of preexisting interests in the media that they are extremely reluctant even to let the media near their operations. By contrast, unattached scholars will generally find that there are no resources available to carry out more nearly objective studies of subjects like this. All in all, then, I have great reservations about the significance of oversight in conjunction with FCMA enforcement operations, though I certainly would not infer from this that we should simply forget about the issue of appraising programs of this sort.

In the end, what does this case suggest about the extent to which "economic regulation serves the private interests of politically effective groups."[76] In general, the evidence from this case lends little support to the view of regulation sketched at the beginning of this section. It is true that the enforcement of FCMA regulations in the North Pacific is characterized by the presence of great leeway for the exercise of judgment as well as the occurrence of extensive bargaining. And I hope I have made it clear that there are several serious problems with the conduct of these enforcement operations. In the final analysis, however, the situation does not appear to take the form of an interaction between parties of unequal power in which "the bargains struck favor those being regulated."[77] If anything the reverse is true in this case. Additionally, those responsible for the conduct of enforcement are genuinely interested in the achievement of compliance with FCMA regulations, though some of their specific failings may well arise from bureaucratic problems or personal needs. And I think it would be hard to deny that enforcement operations in the North Pacific are carried on in a diligent fashion.

Of course it is possible to counter these observations by claiming either that the politically effective groups in this case gained their ends through the initial passage of the FCMA or that these groups can counter developments they dislike in the realm of enforcement by influencing the decisions of the regional management councils set up under the FCMA to manage the fish stocks.[78] So long as enforcement operations are directed primarily toward foreign fishermen, there is a prima facie case to be made for such arguments. After all, the FCMA is a protectionist regime favored by domestic fishermen as a device for restricting foreign competition. The acid test for FCMA enforcement, therefore, will come as we move increasingly toward the enforcement of significant regulations pertaining to domestic fishermen.[79] My initial view of this matter was that it would prove exceedingly difficult to mount a serious enforcement program directed toward domestic fishermen. At this stage in my research, however, I feel considerably less certain about this conclusion. In fact, the future of enforcement operations under the FCMA may produce some extraordinary political confrontations of great interest to students of regulation.

IMPROVING PERFORMANCE

My analysis of the actual performance of the FCMA enforcement program in the North Pacific region is now complete. Accordingly, it is time to focus on the lessons of this experience and to offer some proposals for improving the performance of this program in the future. Here I deal with this issue on the assumption that the basic character of the existing enforcement program remains unchanged. A discussion of several alternatives involving more fundamental changes in the existing program is reserved for the final substantive section of this chapter.

To set the stage for the proposals to follow, a few general observations about maritime law enforcement are in order. We are currently witnessing a rapid expansion in the use of marine areas for a variety of purposes (for example, oil and gas development, deep seabed mining, and transportation as well as fishing). Under the circumstances, it is predictable that there will be a substantial growth of regulatory arrangements relating to marine activities and that problems of compliance will loom large in this realm. In my view, these propositions suggest the importance of giving strong backing to an agency that can develop sophisticated capabilities and expertise across a wide range of maritime enforcement operations. In the United States, the obvious choice for an agency to play this lead role in maritime law enforcement is the Coast Guard. Therefore, I believe there is much to be said for the adoption of policies concerning the enforcement of fisheries regulations which will contribute to the goal of promoting excellence in the Coast Guard with respect to the performance of the enforcement mission. By the same token, a concerted effort should be made to induce the Coast Guard itself to increase the importance it attaches to its enforcement mission and to alter the incentive structure facing Coast Guard personnel accordingly. The proposals outlined in this section rest explicitly on these premises.

Training and Incentives

As I have already suggested, there appears to be no lack of will to enforce fisheries regulations among Coast Guard officers. But the training of these officers in the realm of law enforcement is seriously deficient. In fact, most of them lack even the most rudimentary understanding of the nature and role of law enforcement. There is little comprehension of the extent to which enforcement is a managerial activity emphasizing the achievement of relatively broad goals in contrast to an activity conforming to the simple imagery of "cops and robbers." No effort has been made to codify the lessons of experience relating to field operations suitable for the enforcement of fisheries regulations. Admittedly, there is no substitute for personal experience when it comes to the conduct of field operations. But it would certainly be feasible to develop a training program in this area relying on the knowledge of experienced personnel as well as brief training missions in the field. Similarly, there is little sophistication concerning the relationships between field operations and the legal issues that arise in conjunction with enforcement incidents. While I see no point in making individual officers into legal experts, there are good reasons why these officers should have a working knowledge of the legal issues associated with the enforcement of maritime regulations. In short, I am convinced that there is a need for substantial and well-thought-out improvements in the training of Coast Guard officers who are going to play a role in enforcement operations.

Efforts to improve training cannot be expected to yield

major gains, however, in the absence of suitable incentives. At present, it is hard to pursue a successful career in the Coast Guard as a specialist in enforcement operations. The policy of rotating officers not only frequently but also with little attempt to match interests or experience with assignments only contributes to this problem. To the extent that I am right about the growing importance of the Coast Guard's enforcement mission, it follows that there is much to be said for a policy of recognizing and rewarding enforcement as a career specialization within the Coast Guard. This is not to say that officers should deal only with the enforcement of fisheries regulations or regulations pertaining to pollution control; it may well be desirable for an officer to gain experience with different types of enforcement operations. But the development of a cadre of enforcement specialists, who could expect to be able to pursue successful careers within the Coast Guard on this basis, would help considerably to alleviate the current problems of the Coast Guard in the realm of enforcement.[80]

Turning to the specific case of enforcing fisheries regulations in the North Pacific region, I would propose the creation of a joint Coast Guard/NMFS enforcement team located in Kodiak or Juneau. This would be a group of experienced professionals, capable of bringing trained judgment to bear on enforcement incidents on a case-by-case basis. While members of this team would not necessarily accompany every enforcement patrol, they would give regular briefings for officers going on patrol and be available for consultation at all times and for airlifting to the scene of specific incidents in case of need. In my judgment, this would go far toward eliminating the coordination problem discussed above, and it should make some contribution toward achieving the goal of handling like cases on an equal basis. In the process, it would offer a method of transcending the splits between Juneau and Kodiak that surface with some regularity under the existing arrangements.

NMFS Agents

The National Marine Fisheries Service maintains several groups of resident agents in the North Pacific region. And section 311 of the FCMA clearly implies that there is to be considerable coordination between these agents and the Coast Guard in the conduct of enforcement operations. At present, however, NMFS agents accompany only about 30 percent of ALPAT's surface patrols. Additionally, there are serious ambiguities concerning the position of the NMFS agent on an ALPAT patrol. Typically, the NMFS agent has far more experience and expertise regarding the relevant fisheries than the Coast Guard officers on the patrol. Nonetheless, the agent has no formal authority in the enforcement operation; the Coast Guard retains all authority throughout the proceedings. Thus, NMFS agents lack authority even in working with inexperienced, junior officers in the course of actual boardings. Though this may generate few problems if the captain of the vessel and the NMFS agent know each other and get along well, the resultant situation is far from ideal.

In this connection, I would propose that NMFS agents accompany at least two-thirds of ALPAT patrols and that these agents be accorded a much more formal position of authority in the enforcement operation. This would have several advantages. The NMFS agents are generally trained law enforcement officers who tend to have a pretty clear understanding of the basic managerial objectives underlying FCMA enforcement operations. As things stand, they often act to curb the tendency toward overzealousness on the part of Coast Guard officers, and the acquisition of some formal authority would allow them to perform this function more effectively. Moreover, the NMFS agents can remain in the North Pacific region long enough to acquire an in-depth knowledge of local conditions.[81] Consequently, their presence can be used to offset the inexperience of many Coast Guard officers, at least regarding the details of the North

Pacific fisheries. In time, the acceptance of the proposals outlined above in the discussion of training might mitigate the need for NMFS agents on the ALPAT patrols, but I do not think it would eliminate this need. There is simply no substitute for the in-depth knowledge of the local fisheries which comes from working continuously in the region. The cost of implementing this proposal would not be great. It would require the assignment of additional NMFS agents to the North Pacific. But the principal expense would be salaries for these agents, a small item in comparison with the cost of acquiring and maintaining Coast Guard equipment. Of course, such a change would involve increasing appropriations for NMFS, and the operation of bureaucratic politics might make the proposal more controversial than it should be.

Advanced Technologies

Could we improve the effectiveness or the efficiency of the FCMA enforcement program for the North Pacific significantly through the introduction of more sophisticated technologies? There has been ample discussion of a variety of options in this connection (for example, remote-sensing devices, sophisticated radars, electromagnetic intercept techniques).[82] In general, however, I am highly skeptical concerning the utility of this approach to the problem. I do not wish to imply that technology is unimportant in the realm of law enforcement. Nevertheless, I do not think the core of the enforcement problem, at least in the North Pacific, is technological. With respect to the most important types of violations, it is hard to come up with any substitute for visual inspections. I have been highly impressed with the importance of trained and experienced human judgment in dealing with the enforcement of fisheries regulations in contrast to the contribution of sophisticated technologies. The human mind has a capacity for arriving at gestalt judgments which no technological device can match. Moreover, it is remarkably inexpensive to hire and train agents or officers compared to the cost of acquiring and deploying sophisticated technologies.

The one technological development that does strike me as worth exploring systematically in conjunction with the enforcement of fisheries regulations in the North Pacific is the use of transponders. Briefly, ''A transponder is an active beacon which can be used in conjunction with radar or other electronic transmission system to enhance the detection and location of foreign fishing vessels.''[83] Statutory authority to require the installation of transponders on foreign fishing vessels already exists in the language of section 201(c)(2)(C) of the FCMA. The great virtue of transponders is that they would make it possible to monitor the disposition of the fishing fleet on a continuous basis. Under the circumstances, fleet disposition reports could be updated continuously, and it would be relatively easy to check for violations of regulations dealing with seasons and geographical closing lines. Note also that this development would reduce the need for aerial surveillance of the type currently employed. While only experience can determine the precise extent of this reduction, I would judge it to be substantial.[84]

The drawbacks of transponders in the North Pacific relate to their cost and to the possibility of evasion. At this stage in their development, the use of transponders on a large scale may still be unduly expensive. While a large proportion of the cost could undoubtedly be shifted to the operators of the fishing vessels, this hardly eliminates the problem from the point of view of efficiency much less from the point of view of equity. The problem of evasion can be described as follows. Would transponders turn out to be like catalytic converters on private automobiles, which can be disabled easily and whose operation on a continuous basis poses a massive compliance problem? Or would it be relatively easy to deter fishermen from tampering with the operation of this equipment? I have no expertise on this subject, but my sense is that the catalytic converter scenario would not apply. It would be possible to require vessels to demonstrate that their transponders are operative at the time they check in to the fishery conservation zone. Any vessel whose transponder ceased to function in the absence of a checkout message would immediately arouse suspicion. And violations of regulations relating to transponders could carry stiff penalties. Leaving aside the issue of costs, therefore, it seems to me that transponders have considerable potential as an aid to FCMA enforcement operations in the North Pacific.

Enforcement "Style"

Relations between subjects and those responsible for enforcement are tricky under the best of circumstances. It must be assumed that subjects are law-abiding fishermen unless and until actual evidence of the occurrence of violations surfaces. Subjects therefore have a right to expect courteous and respectful treatment. By the same token, it is important for enforcemment personnel to avoid excessive friendliness with subjects. While courtesy is essential, fraternizing with those being inspected can only compromise the integrity of the enforcement program. In the case of efforts to enforce fisheries regulations in the North Pacific, two additional considerations of this type are noteworthy. Under the existing system, enforcement boardings involve conducting searches without warrants, and they may lead to the seizure of vessels without preliminary hearings. This makes it especially crucial to maintain a high level of sensitivity to the feelings and concerns of individual subjects. Further, the subjects are typically foreign nationals whose cultural backgrounds differ radically from those of the enforcers and who may well have very different conceptions of the nature of enforcement operations. Though it is certainly important not to allow subjects to feign incomprehension of fisheries regulations as a consequence of cultural differences, a lack of sensitivity to these cultural variations can be highly unfortunate.

For the most part, the FCMA enforcement program in

the North Pacific gets pretty good marks on enforcement "style." In fact, given the deficiencies in the training of most enforcement personnel, the results have been remarkably good. Nonetheless, there is room for improvement along these lines. Perhaps the most striking case in point concerns language capabilities. While individual patrol units are supposed to carry Japanese-speaking and Russian-speaking officers (Korean speakers are few and far between), there are severe problems in this realm. Language skills are frequently nil, and they are seldom adequate for effective use in complex enforcement situations. In my judgment, greatly improved language proficiency would not only be desirable in terms of enforcement "style," it would also contribute to increasing the effectiveness of enforcement boardings in many cases. Comparatively speaking, moreover, improvement in this area would not be expensive. Therefore, I would strongly support a concerted effort to improve substantially the language capabilities of enforcement units in the field.

But this is not the only area in which there is room for improvements with respect to enforcement "style." In general, every effort should be made to respect the practices of those in charge of target vessels, so long as this does not compromise the effectiveness of the enforcement effort. To illustrate, it is helpful to remove one's shoes upon entering the pilot house of a Japanese vessel, and it is desirable not to remain aboard a vessel for an excessive length of time merely to satisfy general curiosity (for example, to observe the fishing operations over a long period).

Simple Presence vs. Boarding

Could we afford to cut down on the frequency of actual boardings, relying on the mere presence of patrol units among the vessels of the fleet to deter violations? Such proposals will appeal to those concerned about the danger of infringing civil rights as a result of employing current enforcement practices, the occurrence of unnecessary harassment reducing the efficiency of fishing operations, or the amount of time and effort consumed in lengthy boarding procedures. But these concerns must be balanced against other considerations. While the mere presence of enforcement units can be expected to have some effect this impact will dwindle rapidly if it becomes known that presence is seldom followed up by actual boarding. Additionally, it is hard to avoid the conclusion that the most important violations of FCMA regulations from the point of view of fisheries management can seldom be detected in the absence of extensive visual inspections.

What is important in this connection is not to hit on some precise but ultimately arbitrary formula specifying how frequently actual boardings should occur or just what the balance between simple presence and actual boardings should be. Rather, the goal should be to establish a reputation for vigilance and for knowing just when to board to catch violations. Undoubtedly, this goal cannot be reached without a demonstrated willingness to carry out actual boardings on a regular basis. Equally important, however, is the need to minimize the ability of subjects to predict the behavior of patrol units and therefore to devise novel tactics on a continuous basis. An enforcement operation that can keep subjects guessing and ensure that they do not become complacent may well be able to achieve high levels of compliance without making any effort to maximize the number of actual boardings conducted.

Boarding Procedures

Given a specific resource constraint, is it preferable to conduct a relatively small number of intensive boardings or to carry out a larger number of more superficial inspections? More specifically, what is the justification for the recent shift toward a policy of conducting intensive boardings even if this means a reduction in the number of boardings carried out in the enforcement program for the North Pacific? At the outset, it is important to realize that some types of violations will be difficult to detect regardless of the intensity of individual boardings. This is true, for example, of practices relating to the return of prohibited species to the sea in a timely manner and of requirements pertaining to the transmission of aggregate weekly catch data by nationality. In the case of prohibited species, that fishermen exhibit a high level of compliance with the relevant regulations in the presence of a boarding party tells us little about what they do when they are on their own. The transmission of aggregate weekly catch data, by contrast, requires accurate reporting by officials above the level of individual fishing vessels so that there is no way to guarantee compliance on the basis of practices aimed at individual vessels.

This should not be taken to imply, however, that the intensity with which individual boardings are carried out is unimportant. The case for intensive boardings rests on the need to check cumulative catch logs carefully and to compare the catch listed in these logs with what is actually present in the holds of the fishing vessels. This is a complex and time-consuming task, but it is of fundamental importance in any effort to control logging violations or violations involving the retention of prohibited species. On the other hand, it is possible to arrive at reasonable judgments concerning violations pertaining to gear restrictions, seasonal limitations, or area restrictions on the basis of relatively simple boarding procedures, and the control of violations of these types is certainly not a trivial matter. Under the circumstances, there is much to be said for a policy of seeking an optimal mix of intensive boardings and somewhat more superficial boardings. The extent to which this mix should be altered from time to time must rest on informed judgments concerning the compliance problems of specific regions. In this connection, my sense is that the recent shift toward more intensive boardings in the North Pacific was an appropriate response to prior experiences relating to the enforcement of fisheries regulations in this region. But this does not mean that there

will not be occasion to make further adjustments along these
lines during the foreseeable future.

Structure of Penalties

Is the existing structure of penalties for FCMA violations
in the North Pacific appropriate? Are penalties successful
from the point of view of deterring subsequent infractions?
Are they just in the sense that they are proportionate to the
significance of the violations or equitable in the sense that
they are applied in an evenhanded fashion to all violators?
Interestingly, the FCMA itself offers little guidance on the
question of appropriate penalties. It sets maximum penalties
for individual violations (sec. 308) and for criminal offenses
(sec. 309). But it leaves many questions unanswered concerning the treatment of these infractions, and it offers practically
no guidance with respect to penalties for serious violations
leading to seizures of vessels. Accordingly, those responsible
for the enforcement of fisheries regulations promulgated
under the FCMA have been left largely to their own devices
in this realm.

The most important observation to make about the
structure of penalties in the North Pacific is that it lacks any
clear-cut rationale. No effort has been made to study the
problem on a systematic basis or to lay down explicit formulas
for use in specific cases. The result is that actual practices in
this realm inevitably exhibit an arbitrary and ad hoc character. The boundaries among infractions warranting citations,
violations, and seizures are far from clear. Nowhere is the
methodology underlying the computation of penalties in
individual cases spelled out. And several practices associated
with the application of penalties (for example, procedures
employed in disposing of illegal catches) are highly questionable at best. Under the circumstances, it is hardly surprising
that the process of setting penalties for individual violations
has become a focus of somewhat confused bargaining and
that there are widespread doubts about the legitimacy of the

FCMA structure of penalties not only among subjects of FCMA regulations but also among those involved in the enforcement operation. Recently, there has been a marked tendency to increase the severity of penalties meted out in conjunction with FCMA violations in the North Pacific. But there is no indication that this reflects a change in the behavior of the fishermen, and no coherent rationale for this shift is available. It seems clear, therefore, that there is a compelling need for further analysis and clarification of the structure of penalties associated with FCMA violations. If nothing else, this may turn out to be a critical step in avoiding the dismissal of penalties by the courts in specific cases on the grounds that they are arbitrary and capricious.

Several more specific observations concerning penalties are also in order here. There is some tendency to assume that citations are of little significance. Since they are mere warnings carrying no monetary penalty, fishermen may well ignore citations. But this view is surely inaccurate. I have observed cases in which the issuance of a citation has had a definite impact on the behavior of those operating a fishing vessel. Unquestionably, the citation can be trivialized if those responsible for enforcement issue citations in great numbers for insignificant lapses. But it should not be dismissed out of hand as an enforcement tool. Beyond this, if we are to believe much of the recent literature on enforcement, the probability of violators being sanctioned may be more important than the magnitude of the actual penalty over a wide range of sanctions.[85] This may stem either from the use of expected-value calculations on the part of subjects or from the prevalence of nonutilitarian behavior (for example, it may be shameful to be publicly labeled a violator regardless of the specific penalty). To the extent that this is so, it accentuates the importance of refining efforts to apprehend violators on the high seas regardless of how they are treated following apprehension.

So far, the accent has been on monetary penalties even in connection with gross violations leading to seizures. Admittedly, there is something simple and straightforward about monetary penalties, but it seems to me that more thought should be given to the use of nonmonetary penalties in dealing with FCMA violations. These might include such things as short bans on fishing in certain areas, temporary suspensions of fishing permits, or refusal to renew permits in subsequent years. While the legal implications of using such penalties would have to be investigated carefully, the deterrent effects of nonmonetary penalties might exceed those of monetary penalties in many situations.[86] An important complaint about recent practice in the North Pacific region concerns the extent to which the treatment of violators generates de facto penalties of a severe nature. The most obvious case in point involves the detention of seized vessels in port so that they are unable to carry on their normal fishing operations. Not only are such practices questionable on legal grounds, they may also generate de facto penalties (in the form of losses due to enforced idleness) that exceed the formal penalties finally assessed.[87] Whatever is ultimately decided about an appropriate structure of formal penalties, it seems hard to justify the retention of policies leading to de facto penalties. Finally, there has recently been considerable discussion about the idea of tailoring penalties to individual cases, taking into account the ability of the violator to pay. But this idea has little to recommend it. In the fisheries at least, such a policy would tend to amount to a reward for inefficiency. In addition, it would be impossible to administer fairly. It is exceedingly difficult to make accurate judgments concerning the financial capabilities of domestic corporations, let alone foreign corporations. And the "ability to pay" criterion would constitute an open invitation to the emergence of discriminatory practices in this realm. This is a matter for serious concern in connection with fisheries regulations since the formal provisions of the FCMA itself lend themselves to discriminatory use against certain groups (for example, foreign fishermen).

MAJOR ALTERNATIVES

I revert now to the discussion of major alternatives to the existing FCMA enforcement program. Surely the problems afflicting the existing program are serious enough to warrant a more careful consideration of major alternatives. Here I assume that the basic character of the FCMA regime remains unchanged. That is, I assume that it will continue to exhibit the major features of a restricted common property arrangement and that administrative regulations remain the principal vehicle for translating this regime into day-to-day practice. As I have already suggested, the most important alternatives to the existing enforcement program under these conditions are: the 100 percent observer proposal and the idea of relying more on foreign governments as enforcement agents.

Observers or shipriders are individuals who live aboard fishing vessels to keep track of the fishing operations carried out by these vessels.[88] At least for foreign vessels, the use of an unspecified number of observers is authorized under the terms of section 201(c)(2)(D) of the FCMA. There are two distinct tasks that these observers can perform. They can collect data for use in scientific analyses and managerial decisions concerning individual fisheries, and they can play a role in detecting and apprehending violations of FCMA regulations. In the North Pacific region, the practice since 1977 has been to locate observers on a relatively small proportion of foreign fishing vessels (something of the order of 20–25%) and to emphasize the contribution of these observers to data collection rather than to enforcement. The observers themselves have typically been graduate students in the life sciences recruited under NMFS contracts with several universities and signed on for one or two tours on individual vessels.

Obviously, the 100 percent observer proposal or the idea of using observers as a key element in the FCMA enforcement program would require extensive changes in these practices. It would be necessary to blanket the fleet with observers and to emphasize their role as enforcement officers as well as data gatherers.[89] Under the circumstances, we must assume that the position of observer would be filled largely by full-time professionals rather than part-time graduate students.

How effective would this system of enforcement be? Skillful observers located on individual fishing vessels would clearly possess certain advantages over boarding officers visiting vessels for a few hours on an occasional basis. An observer cannot be everywhere at once, and it is remarkably difficult to be sure that sophisticated violations of complex logging requirements are not occurring. Nonetheless, an observer could keep track of the handling of prohibited species through visual inspections of the catch brought on board. He could check relatively easily on compliance with gear restrictions, seasonal limitations, and area restrictions. And he could make a concerted effort to record the total amounts of different species taken by setting up some system for weighing the catch after the return of prohibited species to the sea.[90] These advantages strike me as substantial enough to make the 100 percent observer proposal worthy of serious consideration.

There are, however, some important problems with this arrangement which deserve immediate recognition. There can be no doubt that a serious effort to use observers as enforcement officers would alter the generally friendly atmosphere currently prevailing in relations between observers and their hosts. It does not take much reflection to recognize the tensions associated with situations in which individuals are under constant surveillance by enforcement officers. Whether or not this would jeopardize the personal safety of the observers, it would certainly tend to breed various forms of covert behavior that would complicate the task of the observers.[91] In fact, it strikes me that there is much room for sophisticated or strategic behavior in a situation of this kind. Not only is it possible to tamper with equipment, it is also possible to doctor records in such a way that the true situation becomes exceedingly difficult to ascertain.[92] Domestic experiences with the enforcement of detailed regulations pertaining to air and water pollution offer some parallels in this realm, and they are not particularly encouraging.[93] A further implication of this set of observations is that a determined effort to use observers for enforcement purposes might compromise the data collection effort that is the current emphasis of the observer program. Problems of reliability, which are present under the existing arrangements, might well increase substantially under the conditions envisioned here. Perhaps this difficulty could be alleviated by splitting the tasks of the observers, recruiting separate personnel for enforcement operations and for data gathering. What this would mean is that all foreign fishing vessels would carry an enforcement observer and that some percentage of these vessels would carry a second observer specialized to the task of data gathering.

Note also that blanketing the fleet with observers would not eliminate the need for ALPAT. Though the presence of enforcement observers would no doubt deter some violations, it must be assumed that their presence would not lead to perfect compliance. And these observers would be severely limited in their ability to apprehend violators, regardless of their ability to detect the occurrence of violations. It follows that they would have to call upon ALPAT units to deal with many violations following their detection. It is possible that the extent of the ALPAT program could be reduced in the wake of a shift to 100 percent observers. But whether this would be sufficient to offset the costs of the 100 percent observer program depends upon a series of computations that are difficult to make in advance (more on these below). At the same time, this situation would introduce several new problems. It would be important to ensure the ability of enforcement observers to communicate freely and extensively with ALPAT units and headquarters personnel at all times. There is some question whether the observers could confidently rely on the use of the ships' normal communications facilities for these purposes. Yet it would not be easy to supply the observers with sophisticated equipment of their own. Additionally, since the observers would presumably be NMFS personnel, there would be a major problem of coordination between them and the Coast Guard officers in charge of ALPAT. I have already commented on this issue in my discussion of the existing enforcement program. But the problem would be more severe in conjunction with the 100 percent observer system. The enforcement observers would certainly have to be given substantial authority in their own right, and it would be necessary to negotiate a "treaty" between NMFS and the Coast Guard concerning the issue of coordination in the field.

What would it cost to blanket the fleet with observers in the North Pacific region? Consider first the direct costs of such a development. I assume that enforcement observers would have to be full-time professionals hired by NMFS at the GS 11 or GS 12 level. Given the current size of the foreign fishing fleet, I estimate that it would take an addition of 150 to 250 observers to implement the 100 percent observer proposal for this region. Assuming a minimum salary of $19,263 for GS 11 personnel and a maximum salary of $30,017 for GS 12 personnel (plus an additional 25% for service in Alaska), it is possible to compute a range of possible direct costs for such a program.[94] Thus, the minimum cost for such a program would run to $3,611,813 while the maximum cost would be $9,380,563. This of course covers only the salaries of the observers themselves. Training, support personnel, and needed equipment would be additional expenses. Though these additional items might be relatively modest, they would not be trivial. Recall now that I previously estimated the direct costs of ALPAT as running in the range of $18 to $19 million. It follows that it would require about a one-third reduction of expenditures on ALPAT to permit the introduction of a full-scale observer program in the North Pacific without increasing the total bill for the enforcement of fisheries regulations in the region. How reasonable is it to expect a reduction of this magnitude in ALPAT expenditures? The answer to this question obviously depends on assumptions about several complex issues. In my judgment, however, the likelihood of such a reduction occurring in conjunction with a full-scale observer program is small.

Additionally, such a program would generate indirect and intangible costs that should at least be noted. It seems fair to assume that the program would lead to some increase in the costs of production experienced by fishermen. This might be expressed in terms of reductions in retainable catch per unit of effort (cpue). Though this effect might not be large, I would judge it to be nontrivial. Next, intangible costs would encompass such things as the deterioration in relations between the fishermen and American officials and the wear and tear experienced by individual observers. In the North Pacific, observers would have to be at sea for long periods at a time, and under the best of circumstances there is considerable stress involved in being the lone enforcement officer in a somewhat hostile environment. While it cannot be quantified, I am convinced that the psychological costs of such an operation to individual observers should not be dismissed lightly. Beyond this, there are indirect costs that can best be described in legal terms. An enforcement program involving continuous surveillance cannot help but raise issues relating to the protection of civil rights, and these issues would ultimately have to be resolved through extensive litigation. Under the circumstances, the 100 percent observer program would not only generate costly legal procedures, it might also lead to serious intangible costs stemming from the erosion of important civil rights.

Several additional points relating to costs are worth commenting upon in this discussion of the idea of blanketing the fleet with enforcement observers. Observers of this type would presumably be hired as NMFS agents so that the costs of the program would appear as items in the NMFS budget. At the same time, the introduction of this program might suggest the desirability of reducing appropriations for the Coast Guard's enforcement program. Consequently, such a shift would raise numerous questions in the realm of congressional and bureaucratic politics.[95] Does NMFS have as much strength in the congressional budgetary process as Coast Guard? Is NMFS more vulnerable than Coast Guard to programmatic manipulation on the basis of sectarian political considerations? Does Coast Guard have congressional protectors who would veto any reduction in Coast Guard's budget designed to reflect the reallocation of functions pertaining to the enforcement of fisheries regulations? Would we end up with program duplication and unnecessarily severe problems of coordination? In my judgment, these considerations raise questions about the 100 percent observer proposal which cannot be dismissed lightly.

Section 201(c)(2)(D) of the FCMA specifically requires foreign fishermen to reimburse the United States for the cost of mounting an observer program. Formally, what happens is that the observers are initially paid by NMFS but these payments are offset through the transmission of agreed upon sums to the U.S. Treasury by the relevant foreigners.[96] This creates certain political problems for NMFS, which does not itself receive payments to offset its expenditures on observers. And there is room for hard bargaining concerning the costs of the observer program and, therefore, the payments due from various foreigners. Nonetheless, one of the major political attractions of the 100 percent observer proposal, in contrast to the existing enforcement program, is that it would be possible to make foreign fishermen shoulder most of the costs of this arrangement. Before embracing the proposal on these grounds, however, note the following considerations. The incidence of the costs of such a program is irrelevant to the issues of whether it produces effective or efficient results.

Even more important, this proposal merely exacerbates some of the equity problems outlined above while doing little to ameliorate the others. As I have already argued, there is much to be said for policies aimed at shifting more of the burden of enforcement onto various groups of fishermen (and their consumers). But an overt policy of increasing the extent of discrimination against foreign fishermen has little to recommend it on equity grounds.

I should like to add two observations of a somewhat more general nature in closing this discussion of the 100 percent observer proposal. To begin with, I am concerned about the fragmentation of efforts in the realm of maritime law enforcement. As I argued earlier, there is a strong case for identifying a lead agency in this growing field, and the Coast Guard is certainly the prime candidate for this role in the United States. From this perspective, I think shifts that would have the effect of increasing the role of NMFS and reducing the role of the Coast Guard in the enforcement of fisheries regulations must be regarded as unfortunate. Under the circumstances, there is a case for retaining and improving the existing enforcement program even if this requires some sacrifice in terms of effectiveness over the short run. Alternatively, perhaps we should explore the possibility of creating a cadre of enforcement observers under the auspices of the Coast Guard. This would no doubt be infeasible given the current training procedures and organizational structure of the Coast Guard. If the recommendations I outlined earlier concerning these matters were accepted, however, it would seem just as reasonable to establish the observer program as a Coast Guard service as it would be to set it up as a NMFS service.

Additionally, a program emphasizing continuous surveillance raises serious questions from the point of view of efforts to maintain and foster traditions of international cooperation in an increasingly interdependent world. In fact, the idea of blanketing the fleet with enforcement observers seems more compatible with a neomercantilist world view than with any concern for international cooperation.[97] The relevant attitudes seem to suggest that it is necessary to divide up the world's resources on the basis of exclusive national claims and then to enforce these claims vigorously against the sustained predations of others. While it is possible to understand the origins of these attitudes, they hardly strike me as a good recipe for effective and equitable resource management at the international level. Of course, comments along these lines might just as well be made about the basic character of the FCMA regime as a whole; the atmosphere of neomercantilism is certainly not confined to the enforcement component of this regime. Nevertheless, an intensive enforcement program involving continuous surveillance of foreigners on the part of American observers would constitute a particularly visible and galling manifestation of the "we-they" orientation that appears to be on the upswing in the realm of international resource management.

Where does all this leave us with respect to the 100 percent observer proposal? The potential effectiveness of enforcement observers coupled with the problems plaguing the existing enforcement program suggest that it would be inappropriate to reject this proposal out of hand. Yet the proposal has severe drawbacks. It would not necessarily yield cost savings, and it would raise large questions in the realm of equity. The proposal might well run afoul of congressional and bureaucratic politics. A large-scale program of enforcement observers could dilute the position of the Coast Guard as the lead agency in the field of maritime law enforcement. And the international implications of a program requiring continuous surveillance of foreign nationals are not pleasant. Perhaps it would be possible to improve our understanding of this option through the initiation of a pilot program. Additionally, the idea of reforming the Coast Guard in such a way that it could gradually develop a cadre of enforcement observers strikes me as interesting. Under the circumstances, I would support a policy of experimenting with enforcement observers as a possible option for the future. But I would oppose any drastic and immediate shift from the existing enforcement program to a system of blanketing the fleet with enforcement observers.

The other major alternative for the enforcement of fisheries regulations in the North Pacific region rests on the idea of inducing foreign governments (primarily Japan, the Soviet Union, and Korea) to play a more active role in ensuring compliance on the part of their own nationals. Specifically, we might endeavor to shift more of the burden of proof onto these governments, requesting that they supply various types of evidence concerning compliance on the part of their nationals with FCMA regulations. To give such an arrangement teeth, it would be possible to make the renewal of fishing permits or even the continued allocation of quotas for specific species contingent upon the regular transmission of this evidence. Formally, this enforcement mechanism could be built into the provisions of the governing international fisheries agreement (gifa) negotiated with each foreign nation under the terms of section 202 of the FCMA.

In fact, this idea is not farfetched. Individual foreign governments (for example, Japan) already have patrol vessels operating in conjunction with fishing fleets in the North Pacific for the purpose of enforcing internationally accepted rules as well as their own domestic regulations. There is some evidence to suggest that these governments have taken seriously their obligations relating to internationally accepted rules, making a significant if not always fully effective effort to elicit compliance with these rules.[98] And the prospect of sanctions defined in terms of the renewal of permits and the continuation of quotas is surely not a trivial matter. Nonetheless, it would be difficult to achieve striking successes in this realm if the United States were to impose this arrangement in a heavy-handed, unilateral fashion and to convey the message that foreign fishing within the fishery conservation zone is to be phased out as soon as possible in any case. It is hard to imagine foreign governments making a good faith effort to cooperate in this realm in the face of a unilateral and highly coercive approach on the part of the United States. Similarly, the idea of being forced to comply with complex regulations without any hope of being able to continue to participate in the relevant fisheries over the long term can hardly be expected to sit well with foreign fishermen or with their governments. Under the circumstances, it strikes me that there is little hope of achieving favorable results from the option of relying more heavily on foreign governments in the area of enforcement unless such a policy is accompanied by some assurances to the effect that foreign fishermen can expect to be able to participate in the fisheries on a continuing basis.[99]

No doubt the principal problem with this alternative lies in the realm of verification. It is reasonable to expect that foreign governments would transmit considerable quantities of data under an arrangement of this type. But how would we determine the accuracy or quality of these data? What barriers would there be to stop each government from manipulating the data to convey systematic misrepresentations or more sophisticated biases? Legal remedies are not likely to offer much help in solving problems of this sort. Difficulties pertaining to jurisdiction and the availability of evidence are legion in cases involving officials from two or more sovereign nations. Accordingly, it would still be necessary for the United States to mount an enforcement program in the North Pacific. That is, the United States would need to make some effort to check on the activities of the enforcement programs operated by foreign governments in the field. This might involve some combination of enforcement observers and boarding operations. It is possible that such a program could be mounted for less than the cost of the existing enforcement program in the North Pacific. It is evident, however, that the achievement of success in such an undertaking would require solutions for some complex problems not only in the realm of logistics but also in the area of international relations. Experience with the issue of verification in other areas makes it clear that this is a highly sensitive matter at the international level.[100] So long as verification can be achieved through wholly national means (for example, remote sensing in the case of arms control agreements), it is often possible for individual nations to accept the results on a de facto basis. But as soon as it is deemed necessary to make use of on-site inspections, the international complications mount rapidly. Such activities typically aggravate sensibilities relating to sovereign autonomy, and they are apt to generate serious strains in relations between nations, whose effects are felt far beyond the substantive issue giving rise to the need for inspections. The result is likely to be a heightened atmosphere of coercion at best, and it may well extend to some form of retaliation or tit-for-tat response on the part of the nation subjected to demands for on-site inspections. Accordingly, it must be understood that the alternative under consideration here could give rise to serious intangible costs in the realm of international relations more generally. This is surely a nontrivial consideration in conjunction with the North Pacific region where the other nations involved include Japan and the Soviet Union.

The idea of relying more on foreign governments as enforcement agents is not as farfetched as it may at first appear. Additionally, it is worth emphasizing that this idea and the other options I have discussed are not mutually exclusive. Thus, there would be nothing to preclude a policy of investigating the prospect of greater reliance on foreign governments even while pursuing other ideas aimed at improving performance in the field of enforcement for fisheries regulations. I can see no ground for rushing into a program of greater reliance on foreign governments, and I do not hold out particularly high hopes for this alternative. Nevertheless, I think the idea is worthy of more systematic study. From this preliminary assessment, I would stress the importance of shaping the incentives of foreign governments in connection with any program of this type by giving their fishermen some assurance of continued access to the fisheries as a reward for demonstrated compliance with FCMA regulations.

CONCLUSION

This case study of the enforcement of FCMA regulations pertaining to foreign fishing vessels in the North Pacific does not serve to confirm the standard criticisms of government efforts to regulate private sector activities. There is no evidence of serious cooptation of enforcement agents on the part of the industry or individual subjects. While this might change significantly when it comes to domestic fishermen, I do not think this will turn out to be a critical problem. The enforcement program in the North Pacific has not been overwhelmed by the political power, financial strength, or legal capabilities of subjects or groups of subjects. On the contrary, the deck is somewhat stacked in favor of those on the side of enforcement in certain important areas. This is true, for example, with respect to the structure of legal rights associated with the existing enforcement program. Further, I have seen little evidence of purely personal motives on the part of enforcement agents undermining efforts to pursue the public interest regarding the enforcement of FCMA regulations in the North Pacific. In short, the standard litany of complaints about regulatory efforts does not strike a responsive chord in this case.

Nevertheless, the problems facing this enforcement program are severe. In fact, they are so great that they pose fundamental questions about the ability of the state to perform coherently in the role of manager for restricted common property regimes. There is no good method of measuring the effectiveness of the enforcement program, and this gives rise to a tendency to rely heavily on dubious surrogate measures. It is difficult in the extreme to make meaningful judgments about the efficiency of the enforcement program. It is even hard to apply the less demanding standard of cost-effectiveness in any straightforward fashion. There are fundamental questions about the extent to which the results of the enforcement program are equitable. Partly, this is a consequence of the treatment of similar cases in an unequal fashion. In part, it stems from the tendency of the program to produce in-kind transfers of a questionable nature. Moreover, there are severe problems arising from the inappropriate training and incentive systems of individual officers involved in enforcement operations. I want to stress that this is a systemic problem rather than a matter of parochial behavior on the part of individuals. But this hardly makes it less significant. Overall, it is hard to avoid the conclusion that these problems raise fundamental questions about the efficacy of the FCMA regime in its present format.[101]

Without in any way detracting from the efforts of those involved in the existing enforcement program, therefore, I would argue that we should begin to examine alternatives that would require changes in the basic character of the FCMA regime. As I indicated in an earlier section of this essay, the options that come to mind in this connection include a shift toward the use of incentive systems rather than administrative regulations and a division of the marine areas into highly protected marine sanctuaries and relatively unrestricted fishing zones. It is perfectly possible that these particular options will seem seriously flawed upon careful inspection or that a study of the problem will turn up entirely different options of a more attractive sort. The point is that the problems raised in this study are sufficient to suggest the need for a wide-ranging effort to think systematically about radically different approaches to enforcement in the realm of the marine fisheries.

Five

The Lessons of Experience

What are the relative merits of the strategies examined in the preceding chapters as guidelines for organizing the actions of the state in the realm of natural resources? What can we learn about this subject from a systematic study of actual experiences? Not surprisingly, there are no simple answers to these questions. This is partly attributable to the complexities of resource management, which make it desirable to adjust strategies to real-world conditions on a case-by-case basis. In part, however, it stems from a serious misconception concerning the nature of the state on which much of the existing work on the political economy of natural resources rests.

THE NATURE OF THE STATE

It is common practice to assume, explicitly or implicitly, that the state is a purposive actor capable of identifying and evaluating alternatives systematically with a view toward maximizing some reasonably well-defined goal or objective (for example, social welfare, the public interest, or the interests of some social class).[1] It does not matter whether the perspective is that of neoclassical microeconomics, socialism, Marxism, or contemporary ecological analysis. They all share this premise, though of course they differ greatly in specifying the content of the goal or objective to be pursued by the state. Admittedly, most analysts treat this premise as little more than a reasonable approximation of reality rather than a perfectly accurate characterization of the role of the state. But this does not eliminate the resultant problems. Except in the crudest of senses, the state is simply not a purposive actor endeavoring to maximize any identifiable value or objective. Rather, it is more appropriately conceptualized as an institutional framework or arena within which social choice processes take place on a continuous basis. That is, the state is a social institution whose principal function is to aggregate the diverse preferences of individuals and groups over a wide range of issues into collective choices for the society at large.[2]

Sometimes a stream of social choice processes will yield outcomes that are consistent with each other or that exhibit a common orientation. When this happens, it may make sense to look upon the state or the government as an instrument moving society in an identifiable direction. For example, it seems justifiable to offer such an interpretation of the set of events known collectively as the "New Deal" in the United States. Those who espouse a Marxian perspective will no doubt argue that some such directionality constitutes a characteristic feature of the actions of the state in most societies.[3] And it is clearly true that asymmetries among interest groups with respect to access and influence typically serve to restrict or channel the substantive content of the outcomes flowing from social choice processes. In fact, however, these outcomes are often remarkably diverse, even in political systems that seem rather hierarchical or authoritarian at first glance. Some groups gain the upper hand in conjunction with certain collective choices, while other interests or factions triumph when it is necessary to arrive at social choices in different areas. Further, such diversity is common even within the same general issue area (for example, energy policy or the regulation of hazardous wastes in contemporary America).[4]

Under such conditions, it remains perfectly reasonable to think of the state as performing important social functions in the realm of conflict resolution or conflict management.[5] But it makes little sense to argue that the state is a purposive actor pursuing well-defined goals and systematically moving society in identifiable, much less coherent, directions.

None of this is meant to downplay the role of the state in the realm of natural resources. It is hard to envision any alternative to the state for the performance of some functions in modern societies (for example, the definition and enforcement of property rights). Like other social choice mechanisms, the state is capable of operating to produce outcomes beneficial to society without performing as an integrated or purposive actor. And it is easy to demonstrate that the results produced by the private sector in arriving at societal decisions about the use of natural resources often leave a great deal to be desired. But these observations hardly justify acceptance of the conception of the state as a purposive actor, which underlies much of the recent literature on resource management. Whatever we assume about the nature of the state, therefore, it would be a mistake to expect a clear-cut and coherent stream of outcomes to flow from the pursuit of any of the strategies examined in the preceding chapters.[6]

SPECIFIC LESSONS

Additionally, an analysis of actual experiences makes it clear that several more specific problems commonly afflict the activities of the state in the realm of resource management. Public policies relating to natural resources frequently produce unforeseen and unintended consequences of a disruptive nature (whether or not the intended goals are reached).[7] Thus, no one appears to have foreseen the severe problems now arising in conjunction with the Alaska Native claims settlement, the full impact of the problem of nuclear waste disposal, or the difficulties of dealing with expanding animal populations currently emerging under the regime for

marine mammals adopted in 1972. Whatever its merits as a
device for resolving conflicts and arriving at collective choices,
government, at least in the United States, is not particularly
adept at using expert knowledge to good advantage or at
considering the intermediate and long range consequences of
the policies it adopts in the realm of natural resources. As a
result, we can expect a certain volatility and incoherence to
characterize the efforts of the state to manage natural
resources, as attempts are made to counter the unforeseen
and unintended consequences of past policies on an ad hoc
basis.

There is also a pronounced tendency for policies or programs ostensibly adopted to achieve some stated goal to be
diverted or captured during the course of implementation.[8]
Sometimes this occurs because the stated goal of the program
or policy initiative simply masquerades the real political
forces at work. In other cases, the problem is attributable to a
discrepancy: the interests in a position to control policy
implementation are quite different from what the line-up of
forces or pressure groups in the legislature would suggest.
Perhaps the classic examples of this sort of problem arise in
the field of regulation, but they are by no means confined to
this realm. Thus, it is no secret that the interests of the oil
and gas industry have played a major role in pushing through
the enactment and implementation of the Alaska Native
Claims Settlement Act. And it is evident that the political
forces behind the articulation of the new regime for the
marine fisheries embedded in the Fishery Conservation and
Management Act have at least as much to do with economic
protectionism as with the conservation or wise use of renewable resources.

Beyond this, the actions of the state pertaining to
natural resources seldom reflect any effective drive toward the
achievement of allocative efficiency. Numerous cases of this
problem have been documented in the literature on pollution
control.[9] But it is easy to locate similar phenomena in other

areas. For example, the United States has never shown much interest in operating the fur seal industry on an economically efficient basis. And some of the provisions of the Fishery Conservation and Management Act run directly counter to the dictates of efficiency. The sources of this problem are hardly mysterious. As I have suggested, the state is essentially an arena for the management of conflicts of interest. Accordingly, it will tend to be preoccupied with questions of equity and distribution rather than allocative efficiency. Of course, it is possible to portray the pursuit of efficiency as a potential source of gains for everyone, but it is important to bear in mind both that this may require a complex and politically infeasible system of compensation[10] and that there is no politically powerful constituency concerned with the achievement of allocative efficiency as such. Since these considerations are intrinsic to the state, especially in nonauthoritarian systems, it is idle to hope that the state will suddenly discover a compelling interest in the pursuit of efficiency as it deals with natural resources.

Yet another specific problem arises because social costs or negative externalities occur with some regularity in conjunction with the efforts of the state to manage natural resources.[11] That is, the attempts of the state to pursue specified goals relating to resources not infrequently lead to disturbing by-products in other areas. To illustrate, while regulations promulgated under the Fishery Conservation and Management Act are no doubt aimed at minimizing serious violations, there is reason for genuine concern when they are used to justify practices such as searching without a warrant, seizing vessels without preliminary hearings, or promoting lengthy delays before releasing vessels on bond. By the same token, it is disturbing to observe the federal government taking actions that are disruptive to the communities of the Pribilof Islands in the pursuit of national or international goals relating to the management of the northern fur seal. It is not helpful to overdramatize this problem; the activities of the private sector in the realm of natural resources are not exactly free from unfortunate social costs. Nonetheless, it strikes me as important to bear this problem in mind in assessing alternative strategies available to the state for the management of natural resources.

In the end, I am left with a healthy sense of skepticism about each of the families of strategies examined in this volume. In my judgment, there are serious and unavoidable dangers associated with assigning the state a major role in this, as well as other, functional areas. But this should not be read as implying any general condemnation of the involvement of the state or the public sector in the management of natural resources. As I indicated at the outset, contemporary conditions clearly make it impossible to avoid a large role for the state in this realm. And the problems that arise when society's decisions about the use of natural resources are handled through the private sector are at least as fundamental as those reviewed in the preceding paragraphs. What is needed, therefore, is a balanced assessment of market failures and nonmarket failures in connection with the management of natural resources.[12] And this makes it crucial to carry out detailed investigations of natural resource problems on a case-by-case basis. There is little doubt that this procedure will yield a complex mix of policies that do not conform in any comprehensive sense to the requirements of one or another analytic perspective or ideological preference. But this hardly strikes me as a basis for serious criticism.

INTERNATIONAL RESOURCE MANAGEMENT

I should like finally to explore some of the implications of my analysis for resource management at the international level. Some natural resources lie entirely outside the boundaries of national or state jurisdictions (for example, deep seabed minerals or the global electromagnetic spectrum). Others cut across national jurisdictional boundaries (for example, highly migratory fish, mammals, or birds). Still others involve extensive activities on the part of nationals of two or more states (for example, many marine fisheries). How should the management of these resources be handled?[13] There is no comprehensive public authority at the level of the international community capable of performing this task effectively. Yet it is increasingly evident that we cannot rely upon some sort of invisible hand to produce desirable results at the international level in the absence of deliberate coordination.[14] The resultant difficulties become especially severe as the natural resources in question are subjected to heavier and heavier usage.

In essence, there are two families of responses to problems of this sort. On the one hand, it is possible to take steps to extend or expand the jurisdiction of individual states either de jure or de facto.[15] For example, the outer continental shelves have already been brought under coastal state jurisdiction to a considerable extent, and the same process is now occurring in the case of the marine fisheries. The principal attraction of this response is obvious: the governments of individual states will often be able to lay down and enforce regimes for these natural resources in a relatively effective fashion. But there are major drawbacks to this response as well. The governments of many states are considerably less effectual than we casually assume them to be, and they are little short of perverse in some cases. Individual states have a tendency to pursue shortsighted or parochial goals like economic protectionism. And the achievement of equity or distributive justice at the international level is likely to be an early victim of this approach to resource management. Under the circumstances, there are good reasons to fear that this tack will breed severe international conflicts over time, though it may seem like the path of least resistance in the short run.

The other basic response to the problems under consideration in this section is to pursue the development of international resource regimes.[16] The essential idea here is not to search for some global solution to the problems of resource management. Rather, it emphasizes the development of ad hoc institutional arrangements for specific natural resources (for example, whales or deep seabed minerals), geographically identifiable areas (for example, Antarctica or Spitzbergen), or specific functional problems (for example, pollution control at the international level). The obvious shortcomings of this response lie in the area of effectiveness. It is hard to induce two or more sovereign states to agree on strong provisions for international resource regimes, much less to give the resultant organizations adequate authority and capabilities to implement these provisions effectively. By the same token, however, this response is not without significant attractions. It offers some hope for the achievement of solutions for international resource problems which are reasonably equitable or just. And it provides opportunities for the evolution of cooperative relationships at the international level. If we are ever to achieve success in building an effective international community, there can be no substitute for a continuous growth of concrete cooperative ventures in a variety of substantive areas.[17]

It is currently fashionable to dwell on the expanding role of individual states in discussions of resource management at the international level. At a minimum, this so-called enclosure movement is now regarded as inevitable on numerous fronts. The postwar period has witnessed an accelerating trend toward the expansion of state jurisdiction, especially but not exclusively in the realm of marine resources. As I have indicated, the outer continental shelves are already largely under the control of adjacent coastal states, and recent developments have gone far toward securing a similar outcome with respect to the marine fisheries. No doubt, we can expect the immediate future to be characterized by the growth of similar pressures regarding deep seabed minerals, marine mammals, navigation, pollution control, and scientific research. Once the concept of exclusive economic zones is accepted in general terms, it becomes progressively easier to expand the jurisdictional content of these zones as each new set of concerns comes into focus.[18]

It is not difficult to grasp the impetus behind this trend. Legitimate criticisms emphasizing the ineffectiveness of many existing international resource regimes (for example, the regional fisheries arrangements) offer a convenient facade for powerful interest groups desiring to extend the control of individual states over various natural resources for reasons of self-interest. In my judgment, however, many of these developments are distinctly shortsighted and dangerous. The effort to devise international resource regimes clearly offers no panacea for the management of natural resources at the international level. But consider the probable consequences of a continued expansion of the jurisdiction of individual states in this realm. Many states or governments are relatively ineffectual with respect to their ability to manage natural resources in any coherent fashion. But this is ultimately the least of our worries with respect to resource management at the international level. The growth of national jurisdictions stems from and contributes to the development of neomercantilist attitudes and perspectives in the international community.[19] Not only is this likely to lead to the adoption of specific policies that are unfortunate (for example, unjustified forms of economic protectionism), it is also apt to encourage the development of postures of confrontation rather than cooperation in dealing with natural resources at the international level. Additionally, this enclosure movement will inevitably create roadblocks in the path of efforts to achieve international justice, distributive or otherwise. This is partly a matter of specific problems arising from such things as unilateral expropriations of preexisting fishing rights. But even more serious is the probable exacerbation by this trend of the broader problems of international justice, sometimes lumped under the rubric of the North-South split. This is so because there can be no doubt that the large, developed states of the North will emerge with the lion's share of the spoils from the natural resource grab that we politely discuss in terms of the enclosure movement or the expanding jurisdiction of individual states. Social systems often exhibit a remarkable capacity to withstand conflict and injustice without experiencing drastic change. This is at least as true of the international system as it is of domestic societies.[20] Nonetheless, the rising tide of interest in the control of scarce natural resources at the international level and the resultant prospects for severe resource conflicts during the foreseeable future strike me as worrisome problems. Barring some significant shifts in present trends, we may find ourselves on a collision course that will lead to highly disruptive and even violent confrontations from which no individual state will emerge as a victor. Therefore, I should like to conclude with a modest plea for a reconsideration of the bases of the current trend toward expanding the jurisdiction of individual states over natural resources. Though international resource regimes are afflicted with numerous problems, a progressive abandonment of cooperative arrangements along these lines may lead to far more destructive outcomes within the foreseeable future.

Notes

1. The Role of the State

1. For exact figures on the ownership of land in America see Peter Meyer, "Land Rush: A Survey of America's Land," *Harper's* 258 (January 1979): 45–60.

2. Marion Clawson, *Forests for Whom and for What?* (Baltimore, 1975).

3. J. W. Devanney III, *The OCS Petroleum Pie*, MIT Sea Grant Program, Rept. No. MITSG 75–10 (Cambridge, 1975).

4. For a clear-cut illustration see Anthony Scott, *Natural Resources: the Economics of Conservation* (Toronto, 1973), chap. 1.

5. Ibid., p. 37.

6. For a more general expression of this point of view consult Robert H. Haveman and Kenyon A. Knopf, *The Market System*, 3d ed. (New York, 1978), pp. 230–268.

7. This orientation can be traced at least to John Locke's essay entitled *The Second Treatise of Government* written in the seventeenth century.

8. Scott, *Natural Resources*, p. 128.

9. Barry Commoner, *The Closing Circle* (New York, 1971), esp. pp. 29–35.

10. Ibid., p. 124.

11. For an early but powerful expression of this position see K. William Kapp, *The Social Costs of Private Enterprise* (New York, 1971).

12. The seminal modern essay on these barriers is Mancur Olson, Jr., *The Logic of Collective Action* (Cambridge, 1965).

13. For a clear statement see Paul R. Ehrlich et al., *Ecoscience: Population, Resources, Environment* (San Francisco, 1977), esp. chap. 1.

14. A significant exception to this generalization is Harold and Margaret Sprout, *The Context of Environmental Politics* (Lexington, 1978).

15. See also Charles A. Reich, "The New Property," *Yale Law Journal* 73 (1964): 733–787.

16. For a particularly strong expression of this point of view see Milton Friedman, *Capitalism and Freedom* (Chicago, 1962), esp. pp. 1–36.

17. See Samuel P. Hays, *Conservation and the Gospel of Efficiency* (New York, 1975).

18. Consult Clawson, *Forests for Whom,* and Kenneth Dam, *Oil Resources* (Chicago, 1976).

19. For extensive background on this issue see Robert D. Arnold et al., *Alaska Native Land Claims* (Anchorage, 1976).

20. It may be argued that it is inappropriate to treat this case as a simple matter of devolution. Since the "aboriginal" rights of the Native peoples of Alaska had never been extinguished, the Settlement Act can be construed as an exchange of rights between the federal government and the Native peoples. Several considerations, however, militate against such an interpretation of this case. The Treaty of Cession conveys the territory of Alaska to the United States in a fashion that is described as "free and unencumbered" (Art. VI). It makes no mention of Native claims to land or natural resources. Unextinguished Native claims abound in other parts of the United States but this has not prevented the federal government from transferring land and other natural resources to private actors under the terms of a variety of programs. The federal government administered the lands of Alaska as part of the public domain during the decades following the conclusion of the treaty of 1867. And above all, the Settlement Act is not a contract or a treaty; it is a policy promulgated unilaterally by the federal government of the United States.

21. For a discussion of issues arising in connection with Native claims in northern Canada see the report of the Berger Commission: Thomas Berger, *Northern Frontier, Northern Homeland,* vol. 1 (Toronto, 1977).

22. Oskar Lange and Fred M. Taylor, *On the Economic Theory of Socialism* (Minneapolis, 1938).

23. Anthony Sampson, *The Seven Sisters* (New York, 1975), esp. pp. 238–240 and 332–333.

24. See also Charles E. Lindblom, *Politics and Markets* (New York, 1977), esp. parts 6 and 7.

25. See U.S. Department of Commerce, "The Story of the Pribilof Fur Seals" (Washington, 1977).

26. This is the successor to the original Fur Seal Treaty of 1911. The text of the 1957 Convention can be found at TIAS 3948 or 8 UST 2282.

27. Specifically, it originated with the Fur Seal Act of 1910 (PL 61–146, 36 Stat. 326).

28. See also Allen V. Kneese, "Natural Resources Policy 1975–1985," *Journal of Environmental Economics and Management* 3 (1976): 253–288.

29. Frederick R. Anderson et al., *Environmental Improvement Through Economic Incentives* (Baltimore, 1977).

30. Allen V. Kneese and Charles L. Schultze, *Pollution, Prices, and Public Policy* (Washington, 1975).

31. For a classic discussion consult H. Scott Gordon, "The Economic Theory of a Common-Property Resource: The Fishery," *Journal of Political Economy* 61 (1954): 124–142.

32. On the nature of restricted common property see also J. H. Dales, *Pollution, Property and Prices* (Toronto, 1968), pp. 61–65.

33. For a collection of essays examining this regime from various perspectives see *Washington Law Review* 52 (July 1977).

34. For a more general treatment of the problem of compliance consult Oran R. Young, *Compliance and Public Authority, A Theory with International Applications* (Baltimore, 1979).

2. The Disposition of Public Lands

1. This case study is based on research carried out in Washington and Alaska during 1978. An earlier version of the argument was presented at the annual meetings of the American Association for the Advancement of Science in January 1979. While I have not updated the factual details relating to various aspects of the Native claims settlement beyond early 1979, there is no doubt that the basic problems outlined in this chapter have not been resolved during the interim.

2. It is of some importance to bear in mind that PL 92–203 constitutes a policy promulgated unilaterally by the federal government of the United States. It does not amount to a negotiated

settlement between the Native peoples of Alaska and the federal government. Nor was it ratified in any formal fashion by the Native peoples. This suggests that the Settlement Act is properly construed as an example of what I have labeled "devolution." Equally important, it raises questions concerning the situation that would arise if the Native peoples of Alaska (or some subset of these peoples) should conclude at some future time that the terms or consequences of PL 92-203 are unacceptable. Could these peoples make a persuasive legal argument based on the proposition that they had never formally approved the terms of the Settlement Act?

3. On the concept "machinery of settlement" see U.S., Congress, Senate, Committee on Interior and Insular Affairs, 92d Cong., 1st sess., 21 October 1971, S. Rept. No. 92-405, pp. 80-81.

4. For a helpful chronology see U.S., Congress, House, Committee on Interior and Insular Affairs, 92d Cong., 1st sess., 28 September 1971, H.R. Rept. No. 92-523, pp. 51-52. See also Robert D. Arnold et al., *Alaska Native Land Claims* (Anchorage, 1976), p. 153.

5. The story can be traced in the reports of the conference committee on H.R. 10367: U.S., Congress, House, 92d Cong., 1st sess., 1971, H.R. Rept. No. 92-746, and U.S., Congress, Senate, 92d Cong., 1st sess., 1971, S. Rept. No. 92-581.

6. H.R. Rept. No. 92-523, op. cit., pp. 51-52.

7. The administration's proposals in 1971 were incorporated in H.R. 7432. The text of this bill appears in H.R. Rept. No. 92-523, op. cit., pp. 30-50.

8. For the text of S. 35 see S. Rept. No. 92-405, op. cit., pp. 1-60.

9. See Anonymous, "Village Management Assistance," *Alaska Native Management Report* 6 (15 December 1977): 3.

10. See also Irene Rowan and Lael Morgan, "Alaska Native Corporations: A Status Report," Alaska Native Foundation, 1977, p. 1.

11. Guy Martin, "New Tribes for New Times," Office of Public Information and Publications, Alaska Department of Education, June 1975.

12. But note that sec. 7(j) of PL 92-203 requires that not less

than 10 percent of all funds received by the regional corporations during the first five years of the settlement "shall be distributed among the stockholders of the twelve Regional Corporations."

13. William Alonso and Edgar Rust, "The Evolving Pattern of Village Alaska," Federal-State Land Use Planning Commission for Alaska, study no. 17, March 1976.

14. Martin, "New Tribes."

15. For documentation on the problems of the Native communities see Federal Field Committee for Development Planning in Alaska, *Alaska Natives and the Land* (Washington, D.C.: Government Printing Office, 1968).

16. Martin, "New Tribes."

17. Thus, *The Anchorage Times,* Alaska's leading prodevelopment publication, has printed statements such as the following: "The Natives must use their assets to produce profits. They will want development of their lands as fast as they can bring it about. It is safe to predict that a major part of the future development by private enterprise in Alaska will be on the lands that are owned by the Natives." These quotes appear in Rowan and Morgan, "Alaska Native Corporations," p. 9.

18. H.R. Rept. No. 92–523, op. cit., p. 8. These concerns about the potential political influence of the Natives are also reflected in the striking language of sec. 6(b) of PL 92–203: "None of the funds paid or distributed pursuant to this section to any of the Regional and Village Corporations established pursuant to this Act shall be expended, donated, or otherwise used for the purpose of carrying on propaganda, or intervening in (including the publishing and distributing of statements) any political campaign on behalf of any candidate for public office."

19. There is some ambiguity concerning who is eligible to be classified as a Native under the Settlement Act (secs. 5[a] and 5[b]). For an unusually sensitive discussion of this issue consult Frederick Seagayuk Bigjim and James Ito-Adler, *Letters to Howard* (Anchorage, 1974), pp. 11–13.

20. This provision has led some commentators to worry about the emergence of two classes of Natives: those born before 18 December 1971 and those born after that date. See, for example, ibid., pp. 63–64.

21. Region at-large stockholders are those qualifying under sec. 5 of the Act for membership in one of the twelve regions who are not resident in one of the villages located within the region.

22. See Arnold et al., *Land Claims*, pp. 151–152.

23. On the status of the Alaska Native Fund as of 31 December 1977 see *Annual Report on the Implementation of the Alaska Native Claims Settlement Act, As Amended,* as required by sec. 23 of PL 92–203, January 1, 1977–December 31, 1977, sec. 6(c).

24. Arnold et al., *Land Claims,* pp. 150–151 and Robert R. Nathan Associates, Inc., *Implementing the Alaska Native Claims Settlement Act* (Washington, 1972), chap. 8, p. 10.

25. Thus, "five reservations (Chandalar, St. Lawrence Island, Tetlin, Elim and Arctic Village), which decided not to take advantage of the claims act, took surface and subsurface title to over four million acres in lieu of cash settlement" (Rowan and Morgan, "Alaska Native Corporations," p. 2).

26. For a comment concerning certain ambiguities associated with this provision see Bigjim and Ito-Adler, *Letters to Howard,* pp. 101–102.

27. S. Rept. No. 92–405, op. cit., p. 105.

28. Ibid., pp. 105, 123.

29. H.R. Rept. No. 92–746 and S. Rept. No. 92–581, op. cit., p. 37.

30. Thus, many believe that this provision has sown the seeds of severe conflict among Native groups for many years to come. See, for example, John Hanrahan and Peter Gruenstein, *Lost Frontier: The Marketing of Alaska* (Norton, 1977), pp. 101–102.

31. Arnold et al., *Land Claims,* p. 198.

32. Alaska Native Fund, *Annual Report,* sec. 8.

33. This figure is from the *Alaska Native Management Report* 7 (June 1978), pp. 9–12.

34. For a report on eligibility disputes see Alaska Native Fund, *Annual Report,* sec. 11(b)(3).

35. Thus, "Ten of the 11 village corporations in the NANA region merged with the NANA regional corporation." Similarly, "The village corporations representing the villages of McGrath, Takotna, Nikolai, and Tolida . . . merged . . . to form a single corporation, MTNT, United." See ibid., sec. 30.

36. Arnold et al., *Land Claims,* pp. 160, 277.
37. See, for example, ibid., p. 153.
38. Ibid., p. 198.
39. For a clear exposition of these specific provisions see Nathan, *Implementing the Settlement Act,* chap. 8, pp. 3–4.
40. H.R. Rept. No. 92–746 and S. Rept. No. 92–581, op. cit., pp. 41–42.
41. Note, however, that PL 92–203 does not prohibit the formation of other types of corporate entities among the Native peoples.
42. Arnold et al., *Land Claims,* p. 204.
43. Rowan and Morgan, "Alaska Native Corporations," pp. 6–7.
44. For example, Ahtna, Inc., has eight villages, 1,059 stockholders, claims to approximatley 1.7 million acres of land, and expectations of receiving approximately $12 million from the Alaska Native Fund. Doyon, Ltd., by contrast, has thirty-four villages, 8,805 stockholders, claims to approximatley 12 million acres, and expectations of receiving approximately $115 million from the Alaska Native Fund.
45. Primary sources for these conclusions are Dean F. Olson, "A 3-Year Financial Analysis of ANCSA Regional Corporations," *Alaska Native Management Report* 6 (1 December 1977): 3–7, and several interviews I conducted in Alaska during July 1978.
46. See also Martin, "New Tribes" and Arnold et al., *Land Claims,* p. 293.
47. This controversy, culminating in the removal of John Borbridge as president of Sealaska, was ostensibly concerned with the management of holdings like the Alaska Brick Company. For additional comments on Sealaska see Hanrahan and Gruenstein, *Lost Frontier,* p. 115.
48. Thus, sec. 4 of PL 92–203 is absolutely clear about extinguishing all outstanding Native claims in Alaska.
49. A major source of this need has been the emergence of several complex disputes between Native groups and the federal government over the conveyance of title to land under the Settlement Act. See also the remarks in Hanrahan and Gruenstein, *Lost Frontier,* p. 100–101 on this subject.
50. Olson, "Analysis of ANCSA," p. 4.

51. Ibid., p. 6.

52. In general, consult Alonso and Rust, "Village Alaska." This theme also arose regularly in my own interviews.

53. Of course, they have been able to expand their business operations with the resources flowing from the Alaska Native Fund.

54. Rowan and Morgan, "Alaska Native Corporations," p. 12.

55. Ibid., pp. 10–11. See also the comments in Hanrahan and Gruenstein, *Lost Frontier*, pp. 101–102.

56. See, for example, the discussion in J. W. Devanney III, *The OCS Petroleum Pie*, MIT Sea Grant Program, Rept. No. MITSG 75–10 (Cambridge, 1975).

57. For a wide-ranging discussion of these problems see Federal Field Committee, *Alaska Natives and the Land*.

58. S. Rept. No. 92–405, op. cit., p. 99.

59. For a general account consult Alonso and Rust, "Village Alaska."

60. U.S. Department of Interior, Bureau of Indian Affairs (BIA), *Profile of the Native People of Alaska (Exclusive of the Southeast)* (Washington, 1967), p. 1.

61. On these developments consult ibid.; Alonso and Rust, "Village Alaska," and Arlon R. Tussing and Robert D. Arnold, "Eskimo Population and Economy in Transition: Southwest Alaska," paper prepared for Foundation Francaise d'études Nordiques, 4th International Congress, Rouen, France, November 1969.

62. For details see Alonso and Rust, "Village Alaska," and Tussing and Arnold, "Eskimo Population."

63. For further discussion see BIA, *Profile*, and Alonso and Rust, "Village Alaska."

64. By human costs, I am referring to things like frustration, anomie, alcoholism, suicide, and so forth. See also the comments in Irene Rowan, Margie Bauman, and Lael Morgan, "Alaska Natives: A Status Report," Alaska Native Foundation, 1977.

65. Rowan and Morgan, "Alaska Native Corporations," p. 3.

66. Ibid., p. 8.

67. For example, the bill relating to public lands in Alaska (H.R. 39), which almost passed during the 95th Congress, contained the following widely accepted provision: "subsistence use of wildlife and other renewable resources shall be the first priority consumptive use of the resources on public lands of Alaska."

68. This is partly because of extended delays in formal conveyance of titles to the Native corporations. On the status of land conveyances as of 31 December 1977 see Alaska Native Fund, *Annual Report,* sec. 14(b).

69. This became apparent in the course of the interviews I conducted in July 1978. See also the remarks in Hanrahan and Gruenstein, *Lost Frontier,* pp. 118–119.

70. Of 76,526 regional stockholders in 1974, only 51,899 resided in their own region. See Arnold, et al., *Land Claims,* p. 166 as well as Rowan, Bauman, and Morgan, "Alaska Natives," for further discussion.

71. See also Bigjim and Ito-Adler, *Letters to Howard,* pp. 63, 67.

72. For further discussion see Rowan and Morgan, "Alaska Native Corporations," pp. 4–5.

73. See BIA, *Profile,* and Alonso and Rust, "Village Alaska."

74. Federal Field Committee, *Alaska Natives and the Land.*

75. Nathan, *Implementing the Settlement Act,* chap. 8, p. 31. Many observers have expressed concern that federal or state officials may think about reducing or even eliminating welfare programs directed toward individuals in village Alaska because of the alleged wealth of the Native peoples under the terms of the Settlement Act. Such concerns led, among other things, to the inclusion of sec. 2(c) in PL 92–203.

76. See also Rowan and Morgan, "Alaska Native Corporations," p. 7.

77. Ibid., p. 14.

78. Ibid., p. 7.

79. See Arnold et al., *Land Claims,* p. 284 for discussion.

80. See, for example, Bigjim and Ito-Adler, *Letters to Howard,* p. 64.

81. Rowan and Morgan, "Alaska Native Corporations," p. 16.

82. Ibid., pp. 10–13 and Hanrahan and Gruenstein, *Lost Frontier,* p. 111.

83. On the bowhead whale controversy compare: Rosita Worl, "The Bowhead Whaling Ban," *Tundra Times,* special subsistence issue, January 1978, pp. 6–7 and Philip Shabecoff, "Whale-Hunting Curb is Supported by U.S.," *New York Times,* 21 October 1977, sec. A, p. 12.

84. See Bigjim and Ito-Adler, *Letters to Howard,* pp. 76–77.

85. Alonso and Rust, "Village Alaska," p. 40.

86. Ibid., p. 44. Note particularly the comment that the Mt. Edgecumbe School "has trained an elite which now contributes disproportionately to the most important jobs occupied by Natives, including those in the Native Corporations."

87. See Hanrahan and Gruenstein, *Lost Frontier*, pp. 114–117.

88. An interesting effort to facilitate such communication is Yupiktak Bista, *Does One Way of Life Have to Die so Another Can Live?* (Anchorage, 1975). Yupiktak Bista is a nonprofit organization associated with the Calista region.

89. See Alonso and Rust, "Village Alaska," p. 54 and Tussing and Arnold, "Eskimo Populations," p. 59.

90. For a discussion of this phenomenon see Alonso and Rust, "Village Alaska," p. 54.

91. For example, the new Calista-owned Sheraton Hotel in Anchorage has an explicit program to train Natives from the Calista region in hotel operations.

92. Bigjim and Ito-Adler, *Letters to Howard,* p. 82. For further discussion of these problems see also *Tundra Times,* special subsistence issue, January 1978.

93. See, for example, BIA *Profile,* and Anonymous, "Village Management Assistance," p. 3.

94. Ibid., p. 4.

95. Lee Gorsuch of the Institute of Social and Economic Research, University of Alaska, has studied these problems extensively (for a brief account of his work see Hanrahan and Gruenstein, *Lost Frontier,* p. 112). See also the comments in Rowan, Bauman, and Morgan, "Alaska Natives," pp. 10–11 on village corporation finances.

96. See Anonymous, "Village Management Assistance," for an account of a new program sponsored by the Alaska Native Foundation and designed to improve the management skills of key individuals in Native villages.

97. Ibid., p. 4.

98. See also Tussing and Arnold, "Eskimo Population," pp. 62–63.

99. Alonso and Rust, "Village Alaska," p. 1.

100. H.R. Rept. No. 92-746 and S. Rept. No. 92-581, op. cit., p. 37.

101. Alonso and Rust, "Village Alaska," pp. 54–55.

102. Bigjim and Ito-Adler, *Letters to Howard,* p. 8.

103. For the example of land conveyances see Alaska Native Fund, *Annual Report,* Sec. 14(b).

104. In fact, Congress has passed amendments to the Alaska Native Claims Settlement Act on several occasions: PL 94-204, 2 January 1976; PL 94-456, 4 October 1976, and PL 95-178, 15 November 1977. While some of the changes are not trivial, these amendments have certainly not confronted the principal unforeseen and unintended consequences of the Settlement Act in any meaningful fashion.

105. For a variety of other illustrations consult Milton Friedman, *Capitalism and Freedom* (Chicago, 1962), esp. chap. 11.

3. The State as Operating Authority

1. This case study is based on research carried out in Washington and on the Pribilof Islands largely during 1979. While the factual details reported in this chapter have not been updated beyond early 1980, it is clear that the underlying issues at stake with respect to the harvest of fur seals remain unchanged. For their generous assistance in connection with this study, I am grateful to numerous members of the communities of St. Paul and St. George as well as to Walter Kirkness of the Pribilof Islands Program and George Y. Harry, Jr. of the National Marine Mammal Laboratory in Seattle.

2. St. George Island was discovered by Russian fur traders in 1786, St. Paul Island in 1787. Sealskins have been harvested continuously on these islands under Russian or American administration since that time with the exception of the periods 1806–1810 and 1912–1917. In each case, the break was instituted in response to a serious decline in the Pribilof fur seal population.

3. The text of the 1957 Convention can be found at 8 UST 2282; TIAS 3948. The Convention has already been extended for various lengths of time in 1964, 1969, and 1976. Under the terms of Article XIII(4), however, the Convention will expire on 14 October 1980 in the absence of an explicit agreement to extend or renegotiate it. Though the language of Article XIII(4) might be construed to signify that the parties must indicate something about their desires pertaining to the future of this regime by 14 October 1979,

there is certainly no need to make final decisions before October 1980.

4. To illustrate, consult J. A. Gulland, *The Management of Marine Fisheries* (Seattle, 1974), p. 6.

5. Walter B. Parker, "International Fisheries Regimes of the North Pacific," *Alaska and the Law of the Sea* (Anchorage, 1974), pp. 5–8.

6. See ibid., pp. 4–8 for a brief account of the events leading up to the Fur Seal Convention of 1911.

7. While there may be room for dispute among the parties to the Convention concerning the exact allocation of the bundle of property rights pertaining to the seals, there is no basis for concluding that the Convention allots ownership of the seals to any of the parties on an exclusive basis. On bundles of rights in conjunction with property see Bruce A. Ackerman, *Private Property and the Constitution* (New Haven, 1977), chap. 2.

8. If this interpretation is correct, the federal Court of Claims was wrong to argue in 1954 that the "Seals killed by the Natives were government seals" (*Aleut Community of Saint Paul* v. *U.S.,* 117 F. Supp. 432).

9. This is why proponents of terminating the Pribilof fur seal harvest typically support an American withdrawal from the existing international regime. For a clear expression of this link see H.R. 5033, a bill introduced in the 96th Congress, 1st session, on 31 July 1979 by Congressman Wolff (D-NY) for the purpose of terminating the commercial harvest of Pribilof fur seals.

10. On restricted common property, see J. H. Dales, *Pollution, Property, and Prices* (Toronto, 1968), pp. 61–65.

11. It is generally impossible to differentiate between males and females at sea. At least half the seals struck at sea are never recovered. And it is far less costly to kill seals in the vicinity of their hauling grounds than to mount expeditions to take them at sea.

12. In 1911, Robben Island was under Japanese administration and the Commander Islands belonged to Russia. By 1957, however, both Robben Island and the Commanders were under Soviet jurisdiction, and all commercial harvesting of fur seals has subsequently been carried out by the United States and the Soviet Union under the 1957 Convention.

13. Thus, the primary duty of the Commission is to "formulate

and coordinate research programs designed to achieve the objectives set forth in Article II, paragraph 1'' (Art. V[2][a]).

14. For a particularly clear statement of current thinking in this area consult P. A. Larkin, "An Epitaph for the Concept of Maximum Sustained Yield," *Transactions of the American Fisheries Society* 106 (1977): 1–11.

15. For some time the United States has favored altering the Convention to substitute the concept of optimum sustainable population or OSP for MSY. See "Draft Environmental Impact Statement on The Interim Convention on Conservation of North Pacific Fur Seals," U.S. Department of Commerce, July 1979, pp. 5–8 (hereafter cited as DEIS).

16. The Saint Paul herd numbers approximately 1.12 million animals; the Saint George herd runs to about 280 thousand. These two herds together account for roughly 80% of the world population of northern fur seals. For more detailed data see DEIS, pp. 14–19.

17. Loc. cit.

18. Exact figures on the harvest since 1950 can be found in DEIS, table 14 at C–16.

19. For a characteristic formulation of the official explanation of the herd reduction program see U.S. Department of Commerce, "The Story of the Pribilof Fur Seal" (1977), p. 10. The annual harvest of sealskins is now far below the level sustained for many years before the herd reduction program, however, and it is openly admitted that the reduced carrying capacity of the ecosystem for fur seals is probably linked to the rapid growth of commercial fisheries in the area during the 1950s and 1960s (see DEIS, pp. 21–22). Of course, it is possible to justify these reductions in fur seal productivity and harvests by reference to the provision in the preamble of the 1957 Convention which states that MSY for fur seals is to be pursued "with due regard to . . . the productivity of other living marine resources of the area." But the effect of this is to water down the criterion of MSY considerably as a management goal and to open the door to a wide range of essentially political considerations.

20. The changes are set forth in a Protocol Amending the International Convention for the High Seas Fisheries of the North Pacific Ocean signed at Tokyo on 25 April 1978.

21. DEIS, pp. 25–27.

22. Thus, Article IV(A)(1) of the contract with the Fouke Company reads as follows: "The Contractor shall be paid a fixed price per finished and sold sealskin. The fixed unit price shall be established as the sum of the estimated Contractor's cost per sealskin, plus a profit calculated at fifteen percent (15%) of that cost."

23. For a qualitative description see Barbara Boyle Torrey, *Slaves of the Harvest: the Story of the Pribilof Aleuts* (Saint Paul, 1978). An account employing extensive quantitative data and reaching a similar conclusion can be found in Don C. Foote, Victor Fisher, and George W. Rogers, "St. Paul Community Study," Institute of Social, Economic and Government Research (College, Alaska, 1968).

24. For an unusually poignant description of this situation see the opinion written by Judge Nichols for the federal Court of Claims in the 1973 case entitled *Aleut Community of St. Paul* v. *U.S.*, 480 F. 2d, 831–844.

25. For an account of the powers and limitations associated with this status see Foote, Fisher, and Rogers, "St. Paul Study," chap. 6.

26. See Torrey, *Slaves of the Harvest,* for an account of this history. But much the same picture emerges from the evidence accumulated by the Court of Claims in the case of *Aleut Community of St. Paul* v. *U.S.*, supra (1973).

27. Approximately 8 percent of the expenses of the Pribilof Islands Program is attributable to the harvesting and processing of sealskins. The other 92 percent goes to fulfill obligations in the realms of welfare and general community support mandated under the provisions of PL 89–702. The costs of conducting research relating to northern fur seals are no longer included in the budget of the Pribilof Islands Program. For more detailed figures see DEIS, table 17 at C–21.

28. On the distinction between consumptive (or commodity) and amenity use in connection with natural resources see also John V. Krutilla and Anthony Fisher, *The Economics of Natural Environments* (Baltimore, 1975), chap. 1.

29. At present, there is no subsistence hunting of fur seals in the traditional sense. Some seals are taken annually under government supervision for subsistence purposes on Saint George, but Article VII of the 1957 Convention is so restrictive that it effectively

eliminates ordinary subsistence hunting under contemporary conditions.

30. This view receives explicit expression in the language of Title II of H.R. 5033, which calls for the creation of a Pribilof Wildlife Refuge and a marine sanctuary for seals.

31. For a range of perspectives on this theme consult the collection of essays published in *Ethics* 88 (1978) (2).

32. A strong expression of this type of thinking appears in Richard Flathman, *The Practice of Rights* (London, 1976), esp. pp. 70–74.

33. This argument is often presented in a somewhat dramatic and emotional fashion. To illustrate, see Jack Anderson, "U.S. Has a Seal Slaughter of Its Own," *Washington Post,* 30 May 1979, sec. E, p. 12.

34. For an important discussion of this distinction, which reinforces the proposition that it is fraught with complexities, see Thomas C. Grey, "Property and Need: The Welfare State and Theories of Distributive Justice," *Stanford Law Review* 28 (1976): 877–902.

35. Elizabeth Simpson, "Report on Sealing in the Pribilof Islands, 1967," World Federation for the Protection of Animals (Zurich, 1968).

36. See Anderson, "Seal Slaughter," or Greenpeace, "The Pribilofs—The People, and Fur Seals," mimeographed document from Greenpeace Alaska, 17 May 1979.

37. This point is stressed with particular regularity in the materials emanating from Greenpeace Alaska on the Pribilof seal harvest. But see also Title II of H.R. 5033 on the issue.

38. Thus, sec. 2(a)(7) of PL 94-265 calls for "A national program for the development of fisheries which are underutilized or not utilized by United States fishermen, including bottom fish off Alaska."

39. The idea of installing a boat harbor at Saint Paul has been considered from time to time since the 1960s. Originally rejected by the Army Corps of Engineers as having an unfavorable benefit/ cost ratio, the idea surfaced again in the wake of the passage of PL 94-265, and it has been fueled by the growing controversy surrounding the seal harvest. At present, the Corps is working on new feasibility studies concerning the proposed boat harbor. But it

would not be reasonable to assume that a boat harbor will be available at Saint Paul in the immediate future.

40. DEIS, pp. 14–17.

41. Recently, there have been some unexplained indications of an increase in natural mortality among two- and three-year-olds, but the problem is not regarded as serious at this time.

42. This is an issue about which there is considerable disagreement and insufficient scientific evidence to sustain any definite conclusions. For some relevant comments, however, see DEIS, pp. 14–16.

43. "The annual food consumption for the entire Pribilof Island herd of approximately 1.4 million has been estimated at 1.5 million metric tons" (DEIS, p. 13). By way of comparison, this quantity approaches the annual harvest of the high seas fisheries of the Bering Sea.

44. On the idea of stewardship in connection with man-nature relationships see John Passmore, *Man's Responsibility for Nature* (New York, 1974), chap. 2.

45. To illustrate, see Greenpeace, "The Pribilofs—The People, and Fur Seals."

46. For data pertaining to employment opportunities on Saint Paul prior to 1968 see Foote, Fisher, and Rogers, "St. Paul Study," esp. chap. 5. For the most recent figures on employment in the sealing industry see DEIS, pp. 25–27.

47. Under the terms of PL 92–203, Saint Paul is in the process of taking title to a parcel of land on Unalaska Island. This land includes Chernofski Harbor, a natural harbor with some salvageable installations remaining from World War II. Consideration is currently being given to plans under which Tanadgusix would establish a subsidiary for the purpose of developing a fishing industry based on Chernofski Harbor.

48. For an eloquent expression of the potential and importance of renewable resource industries of this sort in northern communities consult chap. 9 of the Berger Report: Thomas Berger, *Northern Frontier, Northern Homeland,* vol. 1 (Toronto, 1977).

49. The experiences of other communities affected by the rapid growth of industries based on natural resources indicate that this is a very real concern. Moreover, there is a growing awareness of the dangers of external economic pressures among the residents of Saint Paul and Saint George. To illustrate, see the letter from Larry

Merculieff, president of Tanadgusix, printed in the *Tundra Times* of 6 June 1979.

50. For concrete examples see Oran R. Young, "International Resource Regimes," in *Collective Decision Making: Applications from Public Choice Theory,* ed. Clifford S. Russell (Baltimore, 1979), pp. 241–282.

51. It is important to realize that the United States no longer occupies anything resembling the dominant position in world politics it enjoyed in the aftermath of World War II. For a more general analysis of the dangers of unilateralism in an environment characterized by growing interdependence see Oran R. Young, "Interdependencies in World Politics," *International Journal* 24 (1969): 726–750.

52. DEIS, pp. 28, 32.

53. The Draft Environment Impact Statement, for example, simply asserts that "Animals occurring within the United States 200-mile Fishery Conservation Zone (FCZ) would be protected by the United States under the provisions of the Marine Mammal Protection Act of 1972" (DEIS, p. 31).

54. The MMPA allows Natives to take marine mammals both for subsistence purposes and for purposes of creating and selling authentic native articles of handicraft and clothing. Experience with these provisions since 1972 indicates that they are extremely open-ended and difficult to enforce. To put it mildly, therefore, the change would create a situation in which "Restrictions on the manner of taking by natives now imposed by the Convention would be eliminated" (DEIS, p. 32).

55. I do not think the willingness of Japan and the Soviet Union to accept the unilateral imposition of the fisheries regime mandated by PL 94–265 should be regarded as evidence that the other parties to the fur seal regime would not object to a unilateral American expropriation of some of their rights in the fur seals. These rights are explicitly protected by international agreement, whereas the case of the marine fisheries was far more ambiguous.

56. DEIS, p. 31. Note also that virtually all fur seals migrating through North American waters pass beyond the limits of the FCZ from time to time, entering portions of the high seas or areas under Canadian jurisdiction.

57. DEIS, pp. 17–18.

58. For a clear, introductory account of the requirements of

benefit/cost analysis see Robert Haveman, *The Economics of the Public Sector* (New York, 1976), pp. 151–171.

59. I was struck by this fact repeatedly in my conversations with residents of Saint George during the summer of 1979.

60. For example, the federal government tore down several houses on Saint George, largely as a way of encouraging Saint George residents to relocate on Saint Paul.

61. Routine monitoring of the seal population continues on a regular basis. But American-sponsored pelagic research came to an end some years ago, and the behavioral studies conducted during the 1970s are now largely complete. Evidently, there are no definite plans for extensive new research efforts relating to northern fur seals during the near future.

62. This would amount to a kind of limited-entry system for commercial sealing. For a discussion of limited entry systems in connection with the marine fisheries see the essays in Lee G. Anderson, ed., *Economic Impacts of Extended Fisheries Jurisdiction* (Ann Arbor, 1977).

63. On the differences between these procedures see Kenneth Dam, *Oil Resources* (Chicago, 1976).

64. See A. Myrick Freeman III, "Environmental Management as a Regulatory Process," Discussion Paper D–4, Resources for the Future, January 1977.

65. Though the critical decision was rendered in 1973 (cf. *Aleut Community of St. Paul v. U.S.*, 480 F. 2d, 831), the amount of the final award was not agreed upon until June 1979.

66. It is worth quoting the opinion of Judge Nichols at some length in this context, *Aleut Community of St. Paul v. U.S. supra*, at 840–841: "Having been compelled to become absolutely dependent upon the activities of the appellee and its agents on St. Paul Island, appellants tell us that they were forced into a state of dire poverty by the abuses of their 'benefactors.' We are told that appellants were deprived of all rights of American citizenship guaranteed them in the Treaty of Cession. They were denied the right to vote, to travel freely, to freely sell the products of their labor, to employ attorneys and to seek access to the courts. Even the internal government of the Tribe was allegedly subverted by the appellee and its agents, deposing native chiefs and selecting new chiefs who would cooperate with the trading company. In short, we are told that the

natives were treated like inmates who had no choice but to do what they were told."

67. That this type of inefficiency occurs is not in dispute. But see also Foote, Fisher, and Rogers, "St. Paul Study," pp. 160–161 for some pertinent observations on the problems created by this situation.

68. Referring to an environment of this sort, Foote, Fisher and Rogers state pointedly that "one fact should be clearly established —that the fur seal industry is in fact to be run as an industry" (ibid., p. 160).

69. Of course, it might prove efficient to conduct sealing operations on the two islands jointly, and it would be perfectly feasible for Tanadgusix and Tanaq to set up a joint venture for this purpose.

70. Under the terms of PL 92-203, Tanadgusix has taken title to approximately 94% of the land area of Saint Paul Island; Tanaq is expected to end up with about 97% of the land area of Saint George (DEIS, p. 9). Note, however, that the subsurface estate of these lands will go to the Aleut Corporation, the relevant regional corporation, rather than to the village corporations. Moreover, the village corporations are not heavily capitalized, and they will have to seek outside capital for many ventures. In this connection, note also that they cannot expect to be able to make use of the recent $8.5 million Court of Claims award. This money is to go to the communities rather than to the corporations, and a large proportion of it is likely to be distributed to individual residents of Saint Paul and Saint George in any case.

71. To illustrate, this system has been employed extensively in contracting for the harvest of timber in the American national forests.

72. There are alternatives to royalty payments for securing appropriate returns to the federal government on the fur seal resource. Several interesting alternatives are discussed in the context of OCS development in J. W. Devanney III, *The OCS Petroleum Pie,* MIT Sea Grant Program, Rep. No. MITSG 75-10 (Cambridge, 1975), pp. 68–95.

73. This is hardly surprising. As recently as 1971, the highest position an Aleut could hope to attain on Saint Paul or Saint George was mixed-gang foreman for the Pribilof Islands Program. What this suggests is the importance of sensitivity on the part of

outsiders in assisting leaders of the corporations to make this transition rather than a propensity to criticize mistakes or to assume the worst about the probable results of local business initiatives.

74. By current standards, the sums involved were always trivial, generally running well under $1 million (cf. DEIS, table 17 at C–21 for specific figures).

75. Efforts to spell out the content of OSP for practical use also make it clear that this concept is closely tied to a management regime (i.e. the MMPA system) under which an indefinite moratorium on consumptive use of marine mammals is the normal expectation (cf. also DEIS, pp. 5–7).

76. Specifically, it would seem desirable to add new language to Article V(4) of the 1957 Convention. At a minimum, this might state that "no decision or recommendation shall be made without explicit consideration of its anticipated impact on the welfare of the local residents."

4. Enforcing Public Regulations

1. For an assessment of the principal approaches to this subject see Richard A. Posner, "Theories of Economic Regulation," *Bell Journal of Economics and Management Science* 5 (1974): 335–358.

2. This assessment is based on two field seasons in the North Pacific as well as extensive research in Washington. During the summer of 1978, I had guest worker status with the National Marine Fisheries Service and sailed with the U.S. Coast Guard Cutter *Jarvis* on fisheries patrol. During the summer of 1979, I sailed with the U.S. Coast Guard Cutter *Munro* under a similar arrangement.

3. On the concept of restricted common property see J. H. Dales, *Pollution, Property, and Prices* (Toronto, 1968), pp. 61–65.

4. These regulations appear in Chapter VI of Title 50 of the *Code of Federal Regulations* (cited as 50 CFR).

5. For a theoretical treatment of the problem of compliance see Oran R. Young, *Compliance and Public Authority, A Theory with International Applications* (Baltimore, 1979).

6. The seminal treatment of this issue is H. Scott Gordon, "The Economic Theory of a Common-Property Resource: The Fishery," *Journal of Political Economy* 62 (1954): 124–142.

7. For general background in this area consult J. A. Gulland, *The Management of Marine Fisheries* (Seattle, 1974).

8. For a broad brush review of enforcement efforts aimed at domestic as well as foreign fishermen see the Comptroller General's Report to the Congress entitled "Enforcement Problems Hinder Effective Implementation of New Fishery Management Activities," GAO Rept. No. CED-79-120, 12 September 1979 (hereafter cited as GAO CED-79-120).

9. For a review of the activities of the regional management councils see the Comptroller General's Report to the Congress entitled "Progress and Problems of Fisheries Management Under the Fishery Conservation and Management Act," GAO Rept. No. CED-79-23, 9 January 1979 (hereafter cited as GAO CED-79-23).

10. Note, however, that the principal fisheries of the region are not uniformly distributed throughout this area. On the contrary, they are concentrated in certain general areas such as along the 100-fathom curve in the central Bering Sea.

11. For background on the recent history of the North Pacific fisheries consult Oran R. Young, *Resource Management at the International Level: the Case of the North Pacific* (London and New York, 1977).

12. For an analysis of pre-FCMA compliance problems in the North Pacific see Young, *Compliance,* chap. 5.

13. See "Semiannual Report to Congress on the Degree and Extent of Known Compliance with the Fishery Conservation and Management Act of 1976," no. 1, prepared in accordance with section 311(a) of PL 94-265, esp. p. 3.

14. The exact content, though not the general form, of these regulations has changed from time to time since their initial promulgation in 1977. On the implications of this change for enforcement operations see GAO CED-79-120, esp. pp. 12-13.

15. But see ibid., pp. 21-22 and 32-33 for a critique emphasizing the lack of dispatch in the disposition of enforcement incidents.

16. See James Q. Wilson, *The Investigators* (New York, 1978), chap. 1 for some more general remarks on the problem of gauging effectiveness.

17. For an attempt to construct a model designed to project future levels of compliance see U.S. Coast Guard, *Study of Coast Guard Enforcement of 200-Mile Fishery Conservation Zone,* May

1976, esp. App. H (hereafter cited as *Study of Coast Guard Enforcement*).

18. Under the circumstances, the only record of infractions would stem from the casual observations of private citizens or government agents on other missions. For a somewhat different conception of the condition labeled "no effort" see ibid., App. H-5-H-6.

19. For a relatively detailed account of the operations of the regional management councils (including the North Pacific Fishery Management Council) consult GAO CED-79-23.

20. See the discussion of this problem in Gulland, *Marine Fisheries*. Consult also P. A. Larkin, "An Epitaph for the Concept of Maximum Sustained Yield," *Transactions of the American Fisheries Society* 106 (1977): 1-11.

21. While I have participated in ALPAT missions (including enforcement boardings), my research has not been supported by any agency of the federal government, and I have had no official status other than "guest worker" during the course of my research.

22. For a discussion of this tendency in connection with traditional police work see James Q. Wilson, *Varieties of Police Behavior* (Cambridge, 1968), esp. chap. 8.

23. For a succinct yet unusually clear survey see Robert Dorfman and Nancy S. Dorfman, eds., *Economics of the Environment* (New York, 1972), pp. xix-xxxiii.

24. The most sophisticated effort appears in *Study of Coast Guard Enforcement*, App. H.

25. For a more general discussion of similar problems see Henry M. Peskin and Janice Peskin, "The Valuation of Nonmarket Activities in Income Accounting," *Review of Income and Wealth*, ser. 24, no. 1 (1978), pp. 71-90.

26. "Semiannual Report to Congress," p. 3.

27. The Coast Guard uses the figures 75% and 25% in dividing effort and expenses between fisheries law enforcement and other enforcement operations nationwide. In the North Pacific region, however, virtually all enforcement activities relate to the fisheries. Since ALPAT relies on units from several Coast Guard districts, I have used cost figures for vessel days and aircraft hours attributable to ALPAT rather than focusing on the budget of the 17th District.

28. See Alaska Regional Office, National Marine Fisheries

Service, "Summary of Current Programs (Fiscal Year 1978)," 1 July 1978.

29. For an analysis that identifies similar concerns in other areas see George J. Stigler, *The Citizen and the State: Essays on Regulation* (Chicago, 1975).

30. It is typically harder to compute benefits than costs in nonmarket situations of this type. On this point, see also Dorfman and Dorfman, eds., *Economics*, p. xxix.

31. See *Study of Coast Guard Enforcement*, App. H-12-H-21.

32. Peskin and Peskin, "Nonmarket Activities," p. 73.

33. For example, illegal Japanese catches have recently been sold at Kodiak, Alaska with disappointing results in terms of proceeds realized. But this tells us little except that the American market for certain species caught by the Japanese is not well developed.

34. For a brief review emphasizing the differences between these tacks see Robert H. Haveman, *The Economics of the Public Sector*, 2d ed. (New York, 1976), pp. 151-171.

35. Consult ibid., chap. 4 on this approach.

36. For a more general discussion of this proposition see Young, *Compliance*, chap. 7.

37. See also the essays in Robert H. Haveman and Julius Margolis, eds., *Public Expenditures and Public Policy* (Chicago, 1976).

38. This proposition is explained clearly in Haveman, *Economics*, pp. 157-158.

39. For an admission of this in an account that is generally favorable to benefit/cost analysis see Dorfman and Dorfman, eds., *Economics*, p. xxxi.

40. This approach is exemplified in *Study of Coast Guard Enforcement*, App. H.

41. Haveman, *Economics*, p. 166.

42. See Allen V. Kneese and Charles L. Schultze, *Pollution, Prices, and Public Policy* (Washington, 1975), chap. 7.

43. See Frederick R. Anderson et al., *Environmental Improvement Through Economic Incentives* (Baltimore, 1977).

44. For recent discussions of nonutilitarian approaches to issues of public policy see John Rawls, *A Theory of Justice* (Cambridge, 1971), and Bruce A. Ackerman, *Private Property and the Constitution* (New Haven, 1977), chap. 4.

45. For a somewhat different formulation of this alternative see GAO CED–79–120, pp. 29–31.

46. See Anderson et al., *Environmental Improvement.*

47. This would presumably involve formal designation as marine sanctuaries under the terms of Title III of the Marine Protection, Research, and Sanctuaries Act of 1972 (PL 92–532, 86 Stat. 1052).

48. For a discussion of this issue in the context of OCS development see J. W. Devanney III, *The OCS Petroleum Pie,* MIT Sea Grant Program, Rep. No. MITSG 75–10 (Cambridge, 1975).

49. Note also that the federal government has been careful not to lay formal claims to ownership of the fish and other living organisms of the fishery conservation zone. While the expansion of coastal state jurisdiction in such zones for managerial purposes is now widely accepted in the international community, formal claims of ownership would certainly not be acceptable at the international level.

50. These fee schedules are currently under review within the National Marine Fisheries Service. It is expected that some changes will be introduced within the near future.

51. In technical legal terms, all of the section 308 provisions concerning civil offenses are described as *penalties.* Only the criminal offenses referred to in section 309 involve *fines.*

52. It is generally admitted, at least privately, that this is an area in which existing rationales are weak or nonexistent.

53. For example, it raises numerous problems in the realm of bureaucratic politics. On this phenomenon consult Graham Allison, *Essence of Decision* (Boston, 1971).

54. These figures are from National Marine Fisheries Service, *Fisheries of the United States, 1978,* Current Fishery Statistics no. 7800, April 1979, p. 42.

55. For a considerably stronger expression of this type of reasoning see Milton Friedman, *Capitalism and Freedom* (Chicago, 1962).

56. For an expression of similar concern about possible conflicts between the pursuit of efficiency and effectiveness see A. Myrick Freeman III, "Environmental Management as a Regulatory Process," Discussion Paper D–4, Resources for the Future, January 1977.

57. Some observers maintain that foreign fishermen are effec-

tively guaranteed a large share of the total allowable catches in the North Pacific during the foreseeable future. This is so (the argument goes) because American capabilities in the area will be slow to grow. Nevertheless, section 201(d) of the FCMA defines the total allowable level of foreign fishing as "that portion of the optimum yield . . . which will not be harvested by vessels of the United States." And the Act itself contains provisions strongly encouraging the expansion of American fishing capabilities (for example, sec. 2).

58. Moreover, the federal government is actively at work on a "new national fisheries policy aimed at tripling the nation's seafood harvest and creating 50,000 jobs" (*Washington Post*, 24 May 1979, sec. A, p. 7).

59. For further details consult GAO CED–79–120.

60. To the extent that such a policy should lead to verifiable hardship for certain individuals or families in the lower socioeconomc strata, the federal government might well want to introduce a subsidy to offset or alleviate this hardship.

61. On the possibility of using a fee system as a method of achieving limited entry, see also Francis T. Christy, "The Fishery Conservation and Management Act of 1976: Management Objectives and the Distribution of Benefits and Costs," *Washington Law Review* 52 (1977): 657–680.

62. Posner, 'Economic Regulation," p. 343.

63. For a clear exposition of this line of analysis see Roger Noll, *Reforming Regulation* (Washington, 1971), esp. chap. 4.

64. A. Myrick Freeman III and Robert H. Haveman, "Clean Rhetoric and Dirty Water," *The Public Interest* 28 (1972): 57.

65. On various images of enforcement consult Wilson, *Varieties,* chap. 2.

66. For a discussion of discretion in the context of traditional police work see ibid., chap. 4.

67. *Study of Coast Guard Enforcement,* App. H–4.

68. Ibid.

69. On the so-called "capture theory" of regulation see Posner, "Economic Regulation," pp. 341–344.

70. Wilson, *Varieties,* chap. 6.

71. For a more general discussion of coordination problems in connection with FCMA enforcement see GAO CED–79–120, pp. 18–21.

72. For a discussion of this option see Stigler, *The Citizen and the State,* esp. pp. 174–177.

73. To illustrate, I was involved in a case during 1979 in which those associated with a vessel seized for gross violations filed an affidavit in federal district court alleging that another vessel had engaged in similar activities.

74. See also Stigler's comments on this topic in Stigler, *The Citizen and the State,* pp. 173–174.

75. The GAO study is GAO CED–79–120. Oversight hearings have been held by the Merchant Marine and Fisheries Committee of the House of Representatives.

76. Posner, "Economic Regulation," p. 343.

77. Freeman and Haveman, "Clean Rhetoric," p. 57.

78. On the composition and decision-making processes of the councils see Giulio Pontecorvo, "Fishery Management and the General Welfare: Implications of the New Structure," *Washington Law Review* 52 (1977): 641–656.

79. For a discussion of the somewhat sketchy efforts to date to enforce FCMA regulations on domestic fishermen see GAO CED–79–120, pp. 7–25.

80. For an indication of lack of enthusiasm on the part of the Coast Guard itself concerning this proposal see the Department of Transportation's comments on the GAO enforcement study in GAO CED–79–120, p. 50.

81. In fact, NMFS has faced problems in retaining the services of special agents over long periods of time in the North Pacific region. Nonetheless, there is a cadre of loyal agents, and it would be possible to take various steps aimed at making these positions more attractive to committed professionals.

82. For a review of these options see Office of Technology Assessment, *Establishing a 200-Mile Fisheries Zone* (Washington, 1977), pp. 45–58.

83. Ibid., p. 47.

84. Reducing the need for aerial surveillance might generate political obstacles to the introduction of transponders on any substantial scale. It is to be expected that the flyers, who are influential within the Coast Guard, would respond unenthusiastically to any significant reduction in their role.

85. For a discussion of this literature consult Gordon Tullock,

"Does Punishment Deter Crime?" *The Public Interest* 36 (1974): 103–111.

86. See also the comments in GAO CED–79–120, pp. 21–24.

87. In the case of the Kaiyo Maru no. 53, for example, operating expenses for the period of enforced idleness have been estimated at $162,625. In addition, it is estimated that the vessel could have caught fish worth $233,814 during this period.

88. On the background of the observer program see Office of Technology Assessment, *Fisheries Zone*, pp. 39–41.

89. There is some debate concerning whether it would be necessary to have an observer on each independent vessel at all times. While the idea of selective observation is attractive from the point of view of keeping costs down, the principal advantages associated with the use of observers can only be obtained by having observers present on a more or less continuous basis.

90. It is possible that a full-scale observer program could even help to overcome the most serious problem with the current enforcement program, the inability to verify weekly catch data submitted by foreign fishermen. To achieve this result, however, would require an extraordinarily comprehensive and thorough observer operation.

91. On these problems see also the comments of NMFS on the GAO enforcement study in GAO CED–79–120, p. 41.

92. This might also lead to problems concerning evidence in legal proceedings. Whose testimony would be accepted as valid in cases where the objective evidence is confusing and the accounts of various parties are incompatible?

93. See the discussions in Freeman and Haveman, "Clean Rhetoric," and Anderson et al., *Environmental Improvement*, chaps. 4 and 6.

94. Note also that the 25% surplus for service in Alaska is not subject to income tax. The effect of this would be to produce a de facto increase in the cost figures reported in the text as a result of a loss of tax revenues.

95. See also Allison, *Essence of Decision*, for a general discussion of these phenomena.

96. So far, observer costs have been paid for out of refunds going to foreign governments in connection with excess payments of poundage fees at the beginning of the year. The costs of a 100%

observer program, however, would certainly exceed the magnitude
of these refunds.

97. For a discussion of the emergence of neomercantilist views in
recent years see Robert Gilpin, "Three Models of the Future,"
International Organization 29 (1975): 37–60.

98. On this subject see Young, *Compliance,* chap. 5, and
William T. Burke, Richard Legatski, and William H. Woodhead,
National and International Law Enforcement in the Ocean (Seattle,
1975).

99. It would be impossible to offer formal assurances of this type
without introducing significant and politically unpopular amendments to the FCMA. Nevertheless, there may be considerable scope
for the development of informal or de facto assurances along these
lines.

100. For a variety of perspectives on this problem in the realm of
arms control see Richard A. Falk and Richard Barnet, eds., *Security
in Disarmament* (Princeton, 1965).

101. That is, the lessons of this case are not particularly encouraging with respect to the efficiency of restricted common property
regimes. While it is obviously impossible to generalize from this
specific case, it does raise some important questions about the
operation of restricted common property arrangements.

5. The Lessons of Experience

1. For more general discussions of this assumption see Anthony
Downs, *An Economic Theory of Democracy* (New York, 1957),
chap. 15, and Roland McKean, "The Unseen Hand in Government," *American Economic Review* 55 (1965): 496–506.

2. The seminal modern exploration of social choice processes is
Kenneth Arrow, *Social Choice and Individual Values,* 2d ed. (New
York, 1963).

3. This theme is particularly prominent among Marxists belonging to the structuralist school. For a discussion of this phenomenon
with special reference to the United States consult Paul A. Baran
and Paul M. Sweezy, *Modern Capital* (New York, 1966).

4. For a descriptive account emphasizing energy policy see David
Howard Davis, *Energy Politics,* 2d ed. (New York, 1978).

5. This is one of the hallmarks of the line of thinking associated with the American pluralists. For a well-known exemplar of this perspective see Robert A. Dahl, *Who Governs?* (New Haven, 1961).

6. For further discussion consult Charles Wolf, Jr., "A Theory of Nonmarket Failure: Framework for Implementation Analysis," *Journal of Law and Economics* 22 (1979): 107-139.

7. For an argument to the effect that such unforeseen and unintended consequences are common in many issue areas see Milton Friedman, *Capitalism and Freedom* (Chicago, 1962).

8. See also Roger G. Noll, *Reforming Regulation* (Washington, 1971) and Richard A. Posner, "Theories of Economic Regulation," *Bell Journal of Economics and Management Science* 5 (1974): 355-358.

9. For an accessible account consult Allen V. Kneese and Charles L. Schultze, *Pollution, Prices, and Public Policy* (Washington, 1975).

10. James M. Buchanan, "Politics, Policy, and the Pigovian Margins," *Economica* n.s. 29 (1962): 17-28.

11. For a more general discussion of the social costs of actions on the part of the state see Oran R. Young, *Compliance and Public Authority, A Theory with International Applications* (Baltimore, 1979), chap. 8.

12. See also Wolf, "Nonmarket Failure."

13. For further discussion see Oran R. Young, "International Resource Regimes," in *Collective Decision Making*, ed. Clifford S. Russell (Baltimore, 1979), pp. 241-282.

14. For a broader, theoretical treatment of the problems involved in relying on invisible hand mechanisms to produce collectively satisfactory results consult Thomas C. Schelling, *Micromotives and Macrobehavior* (New York, 1978).

15. John K. Gamble, Jr. and Giulio Pontecorvo, eds., *Law of The Sea: The Emerging Regime of the Oceans* (Cambridge, 1974).

16. See also Young, "Resource Regimes."

17. For relevant background see Robert O. Keohane and Joseph S. Nye, Jr., "International Interdependence and Integration," in *Handbook of Political Science*, ed. Fred I. Greenstein and Nelson W. Polsby (Reading, 1975), 8: 363-414.

18. See also Francis T. Christy et al., eds., *Law of the Sea: Caracas and Beyond* (Cambridge, 1975).

19. The character and significance of neomercantilism are addressed in Robert Gilpin, "Three Models of the Future," *International Organization* 29 (1975): 37–60.

20. See also Oran R. Young, "On the Performance of the International Polity," *British Journal of International Studies* 4 (1978): 191–208.

Index

Alaska Federation of Natives (AFN), 16, 25

Alaska Native Claims Settlement Act of 1971 (ANCSA), 14–16; as case study in devolution, 8–9; conditions of, 9; and decline of village life, 40–44; and disintegration of sociocultural patterns, 43, 45; divides Alaska into twelve regions, 18; and formation of village corporations, 24–25; individual proposed as principal claimant of, 16–17; legislative history, 15; "machinery of settlement," 15–25 passim, 36–37, 43; and Native lands, subsurface rights, 20, 21–22; and Native lands, surface rights, 20–21; and needs of Native peoples, 36–37; and options for organizational structure, 16–18; organizational structure required by, 15; proposed "modern settlement" of, 17; provisions, 9, 15; regional corporations a key element in, 15–16; revenue-sharing requirement of, 23–24; settlement negotiations and options, 16–18; statewide organizations proposed as key element, 18; unforeseen consequences of regional corporations, 34; villages proposed as key element in, 17

Alaska Native Foundation, 37

Alaska Native Fund, 20, 34–35, 37, 41

Alaska Native Investment Corporation, 16

Alaska Native peoples, cultural disruption of, 42–44, 45

Alaska Native regional corporations: development of sources of revenue, 37–39; disagreements over guidelines for operation of, 23–24; disappointment of Natives in, 36; and disposition of Alaska Native Fund, 20; dominant over village corporations, 24–25; economic choices of, 26–27; economic problems of, 26–32, 37–39; exempt from property taxes until 1991, 23; and exploitation of natural resources, 38–39; geographical regions as basis for membership in, 18; given secondary role in Senate bill, 16, 35; investment goals of, 26–27; key element in claims settlement, 15; lack of Native participation in, 28, 35; Natives as shareholders in, 18; need for experienced personnel by, 28, 39; patrimonialism of, 28; payments to individuals, 34–35; as profit-making business enterprises, 22–23; provided for in Alaska Native Claims Settlement Act, 15–16; revenue-sharing plan required of, 23–24; and socioeconomic problems, 34, 35; and subsistence use of land, 35; and subsurface rights to Native lands, 21–22, 23, 24; transfer of stock in, prohibited until 1992, 23; and urban/rural integration, 40–41; variations in, 26

221